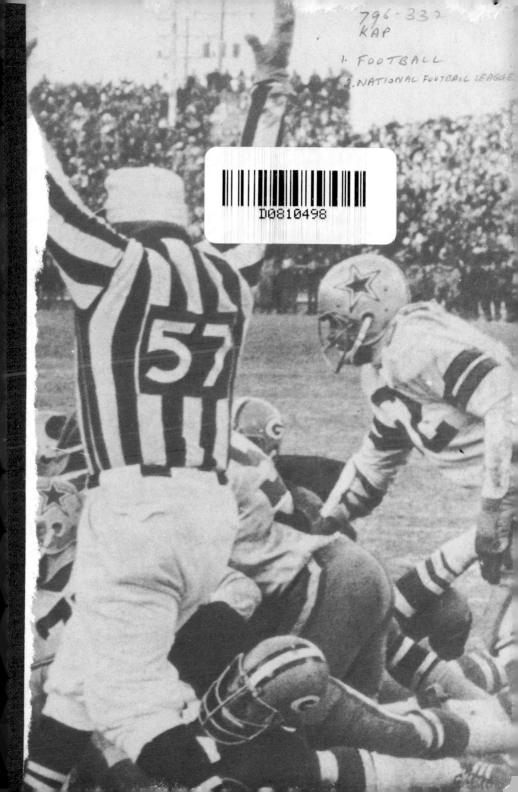

GREAT UPSETS
OF THE NFL

Exciting accounts of ten games in which the underdog fought back to win an unexpected victory.

GREAT

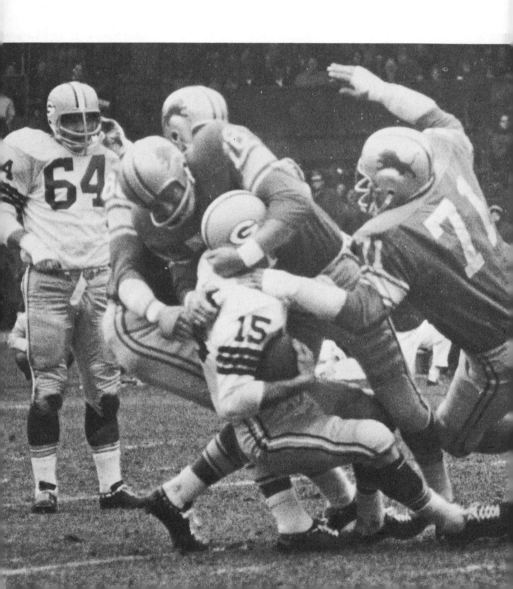

UPSETS OF THE NFL

by Richard Kaplan

illustrated with photographs

RANDOM HOUSE   NEW YORK

7 96·332
KAP

Library of Congress Cataloging in Publication Data

Kaplan, Richard.   Great upsets of the NFL.
(The Punt, pass and kick library, 16)
SUMMARY: Describes ten games in NFL competition with surprising finishes from 1940 to 1971.
1. Football—Juvenile literature.   2. National Football League.
[1. Football.   2. National Football League]   I. Title.
[1. Football.   2. National Football League]   I. Title.
GV950.7.K3   796.33'278   72-1592
ISBN 0-394-82466-0 ISBN 0-394-92466-5 (lib. bdg.)

To my primary receivers,
Julie, Susan and Nancy.

Acknowledgments

Without the help of the National Football League's publicity office and the equally kind assistance of the public relations departments of the various teams—this book would have been extremely difficult to write. And without the skill, courage and will to win of two generations of NFL players, it would have been impossible.

CONTENTS

INTRODUCTION

It is said with pride of National Football League competition that the teams are so evenly matched that, on any given Sunday, any one team is capable of defeating any other—regardless of the standings, or anything else. The history of the NFL is filled with stunning upsets that prove the validity of this "any given Sunday" approach.

The dictionary defines an upset as "the defeat of an opponent that is considered more formidable." But we believe that in football an upset can be subtler than this—and we have given the word a broader meaning in this book. An upset certainly does occur when a team that people expect to lose beats a team that people expect to win. A famous case was the 1969 Super Bowl, when the New York Jets upset the Baltimore Colts. (This game has been described in *Super Bowl!*, a previous Punt, Pass & Kick Library book.)

But other games are not so simple. The Bears and the Redskins in 1940 were considered about even. But the score of that game, 73-0, certainly made it an upset. The Packers were favored to defeat the Cowboys in 1967—and they did. Yet the Packers seemed hopelessly behind with a few minutes to go in the fourth quarter. Their amazing comeback "upset" the Cowboys—even though the favored team finally won. So you see, we have classified as upsets not only games in which the underdog wins, but games in which the favorite prevails in ultra-dramatic fashion—games turned around by shrewd changes in strategy, by thrilling, race-the-gun scoring drives or by a single, last-second thrust that turned defeat into victory.

We do not cite these ten games as the "greatest" upsets of all time, since everyone has his own idea about which was the greatest. Perhaps you have a favorite upset that's not included here. If so, let's hear about it. But we think you'll agree that the games in the following chapters are all great upsets. Read what happened and you'll see why!

GREAT UPSETS
OF THE NFL

1.

MIAMI vs. KANSAS CITY, 1971:
A Foot Either Way

There have been only four sudden-death overtime games played in the history of professional football.

In 1958 the Baltimore Colts defeated the New York Giants 23-17 in the NFL championship game. The winning points were scored after 8 minutes and 15 seconds of the first overtime, when Baltimore fullback Alan Ameche plunged over the goal from one yard out.

In 1962, in the old American Football League, the Dallas Texans (who later became the Kansas City Chiefs) met the Houston Oilers for the AFL championship. The game was decided after nearly 18 minutes of overtime when Tommy Brooker of Dallas kicked a 25-yard field goal.

And in 1965, in a playoff game for the NFL's Western Conference championship, the Green Bay Packers edged the Colts 13-10 at 13:39 of the first overtime period. The margin of victory was a field goal by Don Chandler. Followers of the Colts insist to this day that the kick was no good.

The fourth sudden-death game was played on December 25, 1971, when the underdog Miami Dolphins faced the Kansas City Chiefs in the American Football Conference championship. Before a winner was decided, this contest became the longest ever. It went on and on and on, piling thrill on thrill for the 50,000 fans at Kansas City's Municipal Stadium—and for millions of TV fans that Christmas Day. Finally, after 22 minutes and 40 seconds of overtime play, the issue was settled.

Although both teams had won their way to the championship game, the Dolphins looked like the weaker choice. First, they simply did not seem to match the Chiefs physically—especially up front, in the offensive and defensive lines. Second, the Dolphin quarterback, Bob Griese, had to play despite an injured left shoulder. Third, the game was played on Kansas City's home turf. Fourth, Miami's previous record against the Chiefs can only be called disastrous. The two teams had met six times and Kansas City had won every single time. Fifth, the Chiefs were used to championship pressure—having won five of seven post-season games; the Dolphins' sole championship game came in 1970, when they were unceremoniously wiped out by the Colts.

The way the game started out, it seemed as if the Chiefs would make it seven in a row over the Dolphins with no trouble at all. Kansas City's Norwegian-born place-kicking specialist, Jan Stenerud, booted a field goal from the 24-yard-line to give the Chiefs a 3-0 lead. Then, before the first period had ended, Kansas City shot ahead by 10-0 on a seven-yard touchdown pass from quarterback Len Dawson to halfback Ed Podolak, and Stenerud's conversion.

But just as the first quarter had been all Kansas City, so was the second period a Miami procession. The Dolphins began to move the ball against the powerful Kansas City front four of Aaron Brown, Buck Buchanan, Curly Culp and Marvin Upshaw —and All-Pro middle linebacker Willie Lanier. From the Chiefs' one-yard-line, Miami fullback Larry Csonka, whose 5.3-yard rushing average was the best in the NFL, slammed over for a touch-

Miami's tough Larry Csonka (white helmet, top center) is stopped by the Kansas City line.

down. Garo Yepremian kicked the extra point and the Dolphins trailed by only 10-7. Shortly afterward Yepremian tied the score with a 14-yard field goal. At half time the score was 10-10.

In the third quarter Kansas City went back ahead 17-10 as fullback Jim Otis scored from the one. But Miami countered with an almost identical scoring thrust, as halfback Jim Kiick bucked one yard for the tying touchdown. It was 17-17.

But all this was but a tame preamble for what was to come. The excitement verged on hysteria as the fourth quarter progressed. First it was the Chiefs' turn. Dawson, the great 15-year pro veteran, found rookie end Elmo Wright in the clear and hit him with a perfect pass. The fleet Wright carried to the Miami three before he was dragged down. On the next play Podolak slashed over. Stenerud's third conversion gave the Chiefs a 24-17 lead. In the press box, sportswriters who had to meet close deadlines actually began to write their stories for the newspapers. They singled out the Dawson-to-Wright pass as the play that won for the Chiefs.

But these writers were a little ahead of themselves. In many respects the game had just begun. Desperately but efficiently, Miami fought back. Starting from his 29, quarterback Griese marched his team to the tying touchdown. His principal weapon was the pass—with five completions eating up 68 of the 71 yards to the goal. The final pass went five yards to tight end Marv Fleming with 1:36 remaining in the game. Yepremian kicked the

Dolphin quarterback Bob Griese throws over the outstretched hand of the Chiefs' Curly Culp.

point after, and the game was tied again, 24-24.

After all that clutch effort, the Dolphins were almost undone on the very next play. Yepremian kicked off and the ball was gathered in at the Kansas City goal by Ed Podolak, who played a tremendous game for Kansas City as a running back, pass catcher and kick-return specialist. As the hometown crowd roared, Podolak reeled off a 78-yard kickoff return, taking the ball to the Miami 22. The Chiefs seemed to have victory in their grasp since they had the best field-goal kicker in football, Jan Stenerud. For Stenerud, kicking a 3-pointer from inside the 30-yard-line was considered easy. During the regular season, Jan had scored 110 points—topping the 100 mark for the fifth consecutive season. Only a day before the Dolphin game, he had beaten out Miami's Yepremian as the AFC's all-star place-kicker.

Now, with 31 seconds left in the game, Kansas City's head coach, Hank Stram, sent Stenerud in to attempt the winning field goal from the Miami 31. Stenerud, a soccer-style kicker, made his sideways approach and got plenty of foot into the ball. But, incredibly, the kick sailed wide to the right. It was no good! Seemingly beaten, Miami was very much alive. The Dolphins took possession of the ball and played out the last few seconds deep in their own territory. They were waiting for a chance to win in overtime. As in all NFL playoff and championship games, a tie contest goes into so-called sudden-death overtime—first team to score wins.

At the outset of the first overtime period, Kansas

City once again threatened to win easily. The Chiefs won the coin toss and chose to receive the kickoff. Then they moved the football steadily down the field. When the drive stalled on the Miami 35, in came Stenerud to attempt another field goal. Again victory seemed certain for Kansas City. Granted, Jan had missed one. But even from 42 yards, it was the kind of kick he had made again and again.

We'll never know whether Stenerud would have put the ball between the uprights. The snap from center was high, and Miami middle linebacker Nick Buoniconti managed to get past the Kansas City blockers. Before Stenerud could get his kick up and away, Buoniconti knocked it down. The Chiefs had squandered another great scoring opportunity.

There was only one more scoring threat during that first overtime period. This time Yepremian, Miami's soccer-style kicker, took a crack at winning the game. Garo attempted a field goal from 52 yards out, considerably beyond his usual effective range, and missed it.

All of which brought the game to its thundering climax. With three minutes gone in the second overtime period—the sixth quarter in all—the Dolphins regained possession on their 30. Carefully, Griese called his plays. Five times he used his big, strong running backs—235-pound Csonka (Miami's first back to gain more than 1,000 yards in a single season) and 215-pound Jim Kiick. The two had not been very successful running against the

Chiefs, but now, as exhaustion began to set in on both teams, the Dolphin power backs began to function.

On first and ten, Kiick picked up five yards to the Miami 35. Then Csonka rumbled through a yawning hole in the left side of the Kansas City line and stormed 29 yards to the Chiefs' 36.

"It was a roll-right trap," Csonka explained later. "Kiick and Griese start toward the strong side and I go the other way. The two guards cut with me, and then it's up to me. It was a great call by Griese."

Now the worm had turned. Earlier, the Chiefs had twice had the ball deep in Miami territory, with a chance to win with a field goal. Now it was the Dolphins' turn. Aware of the chance for a field goal, Griese kept the ball on the ground. He sent Kiick into the pile for two yards, then Csonka for four more. On each play the Kansas City players sought to force a fumble, but Kiick and Csonka held firm. On third down and four from the Kansas City 30, Csonka carried again—but was slammed down for no gain by corner linebacker Jim Lynch and defensive end Aaron Brown.

In trotted Yepremian, to see if he could succeed where Stenerud had failed. Yepremian was an unlikely hero. He was born on the Mediterranean island of Cyprus, stood only 5-foot-7, was already bald at the age of 27, and was pro football's only left-footed place-kicker. Garo had broken into pro football with the Detroit Lions, who subsequently dropped him. In 1970, Miami signed him as a free

Left-footed Garo Yepremlan approaches the ball (above) and follows through on his soccer-style kick (below).

agent; the Dolphins, desperate for someone who could kick field goals accurately, figured they had nothing to lose.

Yepremian came to Kansas City determined to prove that he was a better kicker than Stenerud, although Jan had made the all-star team. Yepremian had statistics on his side. During the season he had outscored Stenerud 117 to 110 and had led all NFL scorers. Moreover, as a field-goal kicker, Garo had connected on 28 tries to Jan's 26.

Now Yepremian had to make the kick of his life. It would not be an overwhelmingly long kick—37 yards—but the pressure was terrific. At stake was the AFC title, and much more: the Dolphins might have the chance to go on to the Super Bowl.

Yepremian welcomed the chance to do it himself. "I was dying to get the chance to kick it," he said, recalling the minutes he had spent on the sidelines, watching Csonka and Kiick maneuver the ball into field-goal position. "When we went into the huddle, I just told the guys to give me enough time to kick and not let anyone come through. I knew this kick would make me or break me."

Mike Kolen snapped the ball into the hands of holder Karl Noonan, who set it down just so. Yepremian approached from right to left and got the kick away above the upflung arms of the Kansas City linemen.

"I kept my eyes on the ball and made sure that I had a good follow-through," said Yepremian. "When you do that, you get the ball up—and there's less chance for anybody to block it. When I

The kick is good! Holder Karl Noonan (left) signals the winning score as the defeated Chiefs hang their heads.

kicked the ball, I knew it was going to be slightly to the right, but that it was going to be good. After the ball left my foot, I looked up at the sky and thanked God for giving me a chance to kick it."

As the football soared over the crossbar and between the uprights, every Miami player leaped into the air triumphantly, throwing both arms high in emulation of the official's "good" signal.

In the dressing rooms after the game, the story was Yepremian, of course. He had kicked the most dramatic three points ever. But the story was also Stenerud, who twice had failed. "I have the worst feeling anyone could have," Jan said. "I feel like hiding. It's totally unbearable. My first thought was that I never would go on a football field again." Subsequently, statisticians at the Elias Sports Bureau, which keeps pro football's records, turned up a fascinating nugget of information. During his five-year career with the Chiefs, Stenerud had attempted 206 field goals and made 140—including 74 of 86 from the 30-yard-line in. But never, ever, had Jan tried a field goal from the 31-yard-line—until the one he missed with 31 seconds to go!

Stenerud refused to make any excuses for that kick. "The snap was perfect, the hold was perfect. I just missed it. I've had a tendency lately to get under the ball too much. And when I do, it shoots off to the right. That's what happened. Higher up on the ball, I hook it a little—which I like."

The Chiefs' linebacker, Jim Lynch, who had intercepted a pass and played his soul out, tried to console Stenerud. "You win with forty guys," Lynch told Jan, "and you lose with forty guys."

In the Miami locker room there was no need for consoling words. Yepremian, the little tie salesman, had given the Dolphins the Christmas present they had wanted most. But there were heroes aplenty: Griese, who had completed 20 out of 35 passes; Paul Warfield, the great wide receiver, who had caught seven passes for 140 yards; Csonka, who picked up 86 tough yards on 24 carries, and Kiick, who gained 56 on 15 rushes.

Miami 27, Kansas City 24. Perhaps the game was summed up best by TV commentator Curt Gowdy. "Don't call it 'sudden death,' " he said. "Call it 'sudden victory'!"

2.

NEW YORK vs. CHICAGO, 1934:
"God Bless Abe Cohen"

Abe Cohen.

If you are a fan of the New York Giants, remember that name. Treasure it, even if you haven't the faintest idea who Abe Cohen was.

Abe Cohen never played 15 straight seasons for the Giants. Abe Cohen never built a reputation for championship success in Giant blue. Abe Cohen never threw seven touchdown passes in a single game or ran with the ball for a score. As a matter of fact, Abe Cohen was not even a football player.

Abe Cohen was a five-foot, 140-pound tailor who ran a little shop on the campus of Manhattan College in New York City. And yet Mr. Cohen is part of the Giants' illustrious history—and that of the NFL. In his unique way, he was largely responsible for a victory that gave the Giants their first National Football League title. In the locker room at the end of that game, New York's great halfback, Ken Strong, who had scored 17 points, approached Abe Cohen, who had scored none.

"Abe, you are the man who won this game," Ken said. "You are New York's savior today. You are the man who deserves the write-ups, and if you don't get them, don't be disappointed. True worth is not often recognized in this world."

As the Giants prepared for the 1934 championship against the Chicago Bears, they had little to be optimistic about. They were a good team, but when they met George Halas' Bears head to head, they had almost always lost. The season before, in 1933, the two clubs had met for the NFL title. The Bears had won 23-21 when Red Grange, playing defensive halfback for Chicago, made a game-saving open-field tackle on the final play. And in 1934 the Giants' luck against the Bears had been equally bad. New York met Chicago twice during the regular season. The first time, the Bears won 27-7. The second time, the Bears kicked a field goal in the last seconds and beat the Giants again, 10-9.

The championship game figured to be more of the same. After all, the Bears had won 13 games in a row in 1934 (they were not defeated in their last 38 NFL games). During the season they had led the league in rushing, passing and defense. Their linemen were, on the average, 12 pounds heavier than the Giants', and their backfield averaged 15 pounds heavier per man.

Chicago also had the greatest power runner in the game, fullback Bronko Nagurski. There have been some spectacular fullbacks since Bronko's day—some think that Jim Brown of the Cleveland Browns or his predecessor, Marion Motley, were the greatest fullbacks who ever lived. But those

who saw Bronko carry the ball claim that he will
never be surpassed. He stood 6-foot-2 and weighed
230 pounds. He was not as fast as Brown or Motley, but he ran harder than either of them. He ran
with his head lowered like a battering ram, body
extended almost parallel to the ground. He pre-
sented a very difficult target for the unfortunate
tackler who got in his way.

In 1933 a change in NFL rules had made Nagurski even more dangerous. Before that, a back had
to be at least five yards behind the line of scrimmage when he threw a forward pass. But the rule
was changed so that backs could pass from any
point behind the line of scrimmage. Nagurski
turned this rule to his advantage. He would come
roaring up to the line, where the defenders were
gathered to meet him. But at the last moment
Bronko would stop in his tracks and toss a little
jump pass to an end roaming free in the enemy secondary.

This was the kind of player and the kind of play
the Giants had to face for the 1934 championship.
To make matters worse, the Giants had key injuries. Their outstanding passer, Harry Newman,
would miss the game with broken bones in his
back. Newman's most experienced backup, Stu
Clancy, was hurt, too, as was New York's fine end,
Red Badgro. The Giants were 2½–1 underdogs. "I
know it doesn't look good," admitted Giant coach
Steve Owen, "but we'll give 'em a battle."

Then there was the weather. As has been the case

The great Bronko Nagurski shows his form against the Giants. Above, he prepares to take a hand-off from the quarterback. Below, two Giant tacklers fail to bring him down.

in many NFL championship games, the weather became a decisive influence. Before game time that day, December 9, the temperature in New York sank below zero, and a bone-chilling wind whipped through the Polo Grounds, where the Giants then played their home games. A slick coat of ice made even walking to a street corner a dangerous proposition.

The morning of the game, Giant owner Jack Mara went to the Polo Grounds to check out the condition of the field. A few minutes later he telephoned coach Owen.

"Steve," Mara reported, "the field is just like a sheet of ice. Even the tarpaulin is frozen to the field. I just thought I'd let you know."

When Owen told the discouraging news to his team captain, Ray Flaherty, Flaherty remembered something that had happened when he was playing college football for Gonzaga University in 1925. "We had to play Montana on a frozen field," Flaherty recalled, "and we wore sneakers. We had a lot better traction than they did—and we won the game by plenty. Why don't we wear sneakers instead of our regular cleats against the Bears today?" he asked.

Owen thought it was a good idea. There was only one problem. "Today's Sunday," he said. "Where can we get sneakers on a Sunday? There are no stores open. . . ." Just to make certain, Owen, Flaherty and tackle Bill Morgan phoned all of New York's big sporting goods stores. All were closed.

Discouraged, coach Owen and his team went up

to the Polo Grounds to take on the ice and the cold and the Bears. A quick tour of the gridiron showed that the situation was as bad as owner Mara had said. The playing surface was like a skating rink. The Giant coach headed for the dressing room, where his team was getting ready.

There, talking to trainers Charley Porter and Gus Mauch, stood Abe Cohen.

Cohen was a rabid football fan. He not only ran a tailor shop at Manhattan College, he also made alterations on the uniforms of the school's football team and ran the athletic stockroom. When the Giants played home games, Cohen showed up at the Polo Grounds to help the trainers.

Suddenly Steve Owen knew where he might be able to find his sneakers. Abe Cohen had a key to the Manhattan College stockroom! Owen quickly explained the situation to Cohen. "If our guys had rubber-soled sneakers," he said, "they would be able to get a good grip and maybe go places." Owen asked Abe to rush back to the Manhattan campus and bring back as many pairs of sneakers as he could find. The little tailor hurried off and soon he was outside the stadium, shouting for a taxi under the tracks of the elevated subway line. It was a five-mile trip to the Manhattan campus.

Meanwhile, the game began—with both teams wearing cleats. At first, to the surprise and delight of the 35,059 fans, the home team had the better of it. The Giants were sparked by Ed Danowski, the substitute for passer Harry Newman. Danowski was a rookie who had played for nearby Fordham

University. Mixing his passes with slashing runs by
210-pound Ken Strong, Danowski moved the
Giants from their 36 to the Bears' seven-yard-line.

On first and goal, Danowski went back to pass.
But Ken Strong slipped on the icy turf and missed
a key block—Danowski was dropped for an eight-
yard loss. Now the ball was on the Chicago 15. On
second down, Danowski threw to the Bear goal
line, where Gene Ronzani intercepted for Chicago.

The Bears moved the ball up the field, but then
were forced to punt. Keith Molesworth's kick was
blocked and the Giants took over on the Chicago
30. Four plays later Strong kicked a 38-yard field
goal.

The Giants' Ken Strong kicks a field goal from the icy field.

But as the game wore on, Bear power began to tell. In the second period, a punt return by Molesworth brought the ball to the New York 36. Four plays later, Molesworth passed 22 yards to Ronzani, who went out of bounds on the Giant two. Nagurski smashed over immediately, Jack Manders converted, and Chicago led 7-3. A few minutes later Manders kicked a 17-yard field goal, pushing the Bears ahead 10-3. And to compound the Giants' miseries, Ken Strong twisted his left knee on the following kickoff and limped off the field.

At half time the Giants looked as if they were beaten—physically and emotionally. The ground was so hard that their cleats had begun to break. In the locker room there was only silence as Strong had his knee taped. Not even the most optimistic Giant seriously thought that the second half would be much different than the first.

But then, like the cavalry galloping to the rescue, in rushed Abe Cohen. What Giant muscle had not accomplished, Cohen's enterprise now would. He had brought with him nine pairs of rubber-soled basketball sneakers. "They were all I could find and still get back in time," he said. "I hope they do some good."

The Bears returned to the field first, and Chicago Coach George Halas looked around for the Giants. "What's keeping them?" he asked one of his linemen, Walt Kiesling.

Kiesling had seen a Giant player gingerly testing rubber-soled shoes on the frozen turf. "I think they're changing into sneakers," he said.

Halas reportedly replied, "Good. Step on their toes."

At the beginning of the second half, the new Giant footwear did not seem to have much effect. Chicago's Jack Manders kicked a 23-yard field goal to give the Bears a 13-3 lead. The crowd, cold and disappointed, began to drift out of the ballpark. Owner Jack Mara later admitted, "I was thinking seriously of joining them."

But then the miracles started. With a little luck, a few pairs of sneakers and a lot of determination, the Giants turned the game around. The Giant defense began to stop the Bears. Then in the fourth quarter the Giant offense moved the ball into scoring position.

Danowski arched a long pass toward the Chi-

cago goal. It was headed for back Leo Burnett, but Bear defender Carl Brumbaugh picked off the pass —or did he? Before Brumbaugh had complete possession of the ball, along came Giant end Ike Frankian to wrench it out of his hands. A moment later, Frankian was in the Chicago end zone, completing a bizarre touchdown play. Despite his twisted knee, Strong kicked the extra point and the Giants were back in business, trailing by only 13-10.

Now New York had the momentum. A few minutes later, Strong ran off tackle from the Chicago 42. Deadly blocking opened a big hole, then

Wearing sneakers, the Giants' Ed Danowski (center) runs for a short gain. Another Giant player with sneakers is at the far left.

Strong—his sneakers gripping the ground the way his cleats hadn't—executed a superb cutback past the skidding Bears and raced all the way for a touchdown. Incredibly, the Giants now led 17-13.

Inspired, the New York defense forced the Bears to punt. Again Strong took over. He got the ball on a reverse and went all the way for another touchdown. The conversion try failed, but the score was 23-13, Giants. The underdogs were having their day!

The Bears still could not get proper footing—and the Giants could. An interception gave the Giants the ball on the Chicago 22. Danowski drove 12 yards to the 10-yard-line. Then he took the ball on an end run to score. Bo Molenda kicked the extra point (Strong's knee was bothering him now), to make the score 30-13.

Soon after, the gun sounded and the game was over. The lightly regarded Giants had crammed 27 points into that memorable final quarter. None of them were scored by Abe Cohen, yet in a sense every single one was. Sportswriter Lewis Burton wrote in the New York *American*, "To the heroes of antiquity, to the Greek who raced across the Marathon plain, and to Paul Revere, add now the name of Abe Cohen."

But a New York player, Len Grant, said it more simply. In the locker room after the game, as he was warming his frost-bitten fingers, he said, "God bless Abe Cohen."

3.

CHICAGO vs. WASHINGTON, 1940:

The T Formation Comes of Age

A wise man once said that no one ever attains perfection—he only approaches it. The closest approach to perfection in professional football came on December 8, 1940. On that day the Chicago Bears crushed the Washington Redskins by the score of 73-0 in the championship game of the National Football League.

Many football experts believe that the game was one of the most important in the long history of football. Not only did the Bears score the most lopsided victory in NFL history, they left an historic mark on the game itself. From that 73-0 game on, the game of football—pro, college and high school —was never quite the same.

How could one contest change the game of football? That day the Bears used the T formation. The T was hardly new—it had been experimented with for years, and the 1940 Bears had used it all season. But in the championship game against the Redskins, the Bears added a new touch to the T formation and they used it to perfection. Soon teams all over the country were installing the T and within a few years it was the standard formation in football.

It seems incredible, but the Chicago Bears were actually slight underdogs that day. Washington had beaten the Bears only three weeks earlier and the Redskins had compiled a better season record than the Bears, winning nine of eleven games while the Bears had won eight of eleven. What's more, Washington had the highest-scoring offense in the NFL and one of the stingiest defenses.

The Redskin hero was passer Sammy Baugh. Although he is no longer listed among the ten leading passers in pro football history, many football experts consider him the finest passer ever. Baugh had helped change football himself—he was the first to make passing the dominant offensive weapon of the game. During 16 seasons in the NFL, he won the league passing championship a record six times. In 1940 he was the league's top passer with a completion percentage of 62.1. Sammy was also the NFL's best punter. In 1940 he set a punting record that still stands, averaging an incredible 51 yards per kick. He was also a marvelous defensive safety man (players then played both offense and defense)—a savage tackler and a sure-handed pass interceptor.

Baugh was the Redskin star, but he was not the only standout. Washington had punishing running backs in Andy Farkas, Ed Justice, Jim Johnston and Dick Todd; superior pass receivers in ends Bernie Masterson and Charlie Malone; and powerful linemen in Ernie Pinckert and Wee Willie Wilkin.

The great Sammy Baugh.

Sid Luckman (center) sits next to Chicago's owner-coach George Halas during the Washington game.

The key player for the Bears was Sid Luckman, the first modern T-formation quarterback. Like Baugh, Luckman had been a single-wing and double-wing tailback during his college days. Stocky and almost pudgy, he had played at Columbia, in the Ivy League, which was not famous for its tough football. But Chicago's owner-coach, George

Halas, saw that Luckman was the kind of player who could master the Bears' new 400-play T formation. Halas was planning to spring the formation on the league in 1940. Sid was a good punter, a superlative long passer, a magical ballhandler and an exceptionally clever play-caller.

The Bears, too, had many standouts: fast, strong fullback Bill Osmanski; elusive halfback George McAfee; fine ends George Wilson, Ken Kavanaugh and Hampton Pool; and tremendous linemen such as Bulldog Turner, Danny Fortmann, Joe Stydahar and George Musso. Before the season started, Philadelphia Eagle owner Bert Bell called the Bears "the greatest team ever assembled."

Yet this great team stumbled during the season, losing three games, one of them to the Redskins. That loss was one reason the championship game was so important to the Bears. With 40 seconds to go in the first contest, Chicago trailed 7-3 but had possession of the ball at midfield. The Bears' reserve quarterback, Bob Snyder, completed a pass to McAfee, a great open-field runner, and he darted all the way to the Washington one-yard-line.

Seconds were ticking away, but the Bears were unable to stop the clock legally since they had used up their time-outs. Desperately, McAfee writhed on the ground, pretending that he was injured. The trick worked—the referee called an injury time-out, and the Bears took a five-yard penalty in exchange for stopping the clock, pushing them back to the Redskin six-yard-line.

Hastily, the Bears attempted two passes. Both fell incomplete. Then, on third down, with eight seconds left in the game, another pass shot into the Washington end zone. Waiting to grab it for the winning touchdown was Bill Osmanski—but the ball hit him on the chest and bounced away incomplete as the game ended. Osmanski and coach Halas insisted that a Washington defender had held Osmanski's arms so that he could not catch the ball, committing pass interference. But the officials ignored the Bears' protests and walked off the field. The Redskins had squeezed by 7-3.

The Bears were already angry. Then as they trudged toward their dressing room, they heard some Redskin players shout tauntingly, "Crybabies! Crybabies!" The next day, the newspapers quoted the Redskins' flamboyant owner, George Preston Marshall. "The Bears are not a second-half team," Marshall said. "They're front-runners, quitters. They're just a bunch of crybabies."

George Halas had carefully clipped those stories out of the newspapers. The week before the championship rematch he pinned them to the locker room wall. "I had just the psychological needle I wanted," he said later. "I kept throwing it up to my players that the Redskins had called us quitters and crybabies. They got so worked up I was afraid they would kill the Redskins, not just beat them."

Of course, Halas knew that it would take more than an appetite for revenge to beat Washington. "Papa Bear" disliked the Redskins, but he did not underestimate them. Instead he made painstaking plans for their downfall.

Halas and his assistants studied movies of the Redskins in action, searching for a weakness in the Washington defense. The Bears had been the first pro team to use the T formation, and coach Halas had already added a slight variation. When the rest of the team was set, sometimes a halfback would leave his position and run parallel to the line of scrimmage. This man in motion while the play was beginning confused the defenses and gave the Bears a slight advantage. But then the defenses adjusted. The Redskins had not been fooled—the Bears had not scored a touchdown in that hotly disputed 7-3 game.

Now Halas was looking for a new variation to fool the Redskins in the title game. He called Clark Shaughnessy, head football coach at Stanford University, for help. Shaughnessy was an imaginative football strategist who had taught Halas much about the T formation. Shaughnessy's Stanford team was preparing to play Nebraska in the Rose Bowl, but he came to Chicago to help the Bears prepare for the Redskins.

Halas and Shaughnessy saw from the films that the Redskins invariably adjusted to the Bears' man in motion by sending a linebacker in the same direction. If the man in motion went left, a Redskin linebacker shifted to the same side. The pattern never varied. The two tacticians decided to take advantage of that overshift. They devised "counter" plays—plays that would be run counter to the direction taken by the man in motion. For example, the Bears planned to send their man in motion to the left, then aim a running play back to the right. Halas had used this type of play on and off for 20 years, but he hoped it would surprise the Redskins and give the Bears an advantage.

Only one uncertainty remained. Would the Redskins continue to over-shift their linebackers, thus leaving them open to the "counter" play? To make absolutely sure, coach Halas instructed quarterback Luckman to call an exploratory play the first time Chicago got the ball—a standard man-in-motion play to see how the Redskin linebackers would respond.

The day of the game was snappy (39 degrees) but sunny, with a light wind. Playing conditions were ideal. A crowd of 36,034 jammed into Washington's Griffith Stadium. The Bears were ready. "There was a feeling of tension in the air," Sid Luckman said later, "as though something tremendous was about to happen."

The Redskins kicked off and Chicago halfback Ray Nolting returned the ball to his 25-yard-line. Then Luckman called the first play. Nolting, the left halfback, went in motion to the right—and a Redskin linebacker followed him, just as he had done in the earlier game. Luckman handed the ball to right halfback McAfee, who hit the middle of the Redskin line, gaining seven yards.

In the huddle Luckman smiled confidently. "They're using the same defense," he said. "Let's see what we can do with it."

The legend says that on that second scrimmage

play, Luckman called the first, memorable "counter." But a film in the Pro Football Hall of Fame at Canton, Ohio, shows that it was not a counter play at all. Right halfback McAfee went in motion to the left. Luckman faked a hand-off to Nolting, then gave the ball to Osmanski. But the play was not a counter play; it was an off-tackle slant to the same side as the man in motion.

The strategy was not spectacular, but the play was. Osmanski, nicknamed "Bullet Bill," added a special touch on the spur of the moment. As he headed for the left tackle hole, he saw that it had been plugged by a Washington lineman. So the Bear fullback improvised. With a brilliant swerve to the outside—a "dip," he called it—the 187-pound Bear back turned left and sped down the sideline. At about the Redskin 30, Washington de-

Bill Osmanski carries the ball on the first of Chicago's eleven touchdown plays.

fenders Jim Johnston and Ed Justice seemed to have Osmanski hemmed in. But suddenly Chicago end George Wilson caught up with the play. Wilson's earthquaking block knocked both Redskins out of the play and Osmanski completed a 68-yard touchdown run.

It was sweet revenge for Osmanski—after missing the last-second pass in the earlier game, he scored in the championship contest on the second play from scrimmage. Jack Manders kicked the extra point and the Bears led 7-0.

The Redskins threatened to come back and tie the game in a hurry. Washington fullback Max Krause returned the kickoff 51 yards, and four plays later Baugh had the Redskins on the Bear 26.

On third down Sammy called a pass play from a double wing formation. Baugh sent four pass receivers downfield against three Chicago defenders. He coolly looked for the free man and found Charlie Malone, the Redskins' 6-foot-4 right end, all by himself inside the Bear five-yard-line. The Washington crowd began to roar as Baugh's pass spiraled toward Malone. A game-tying Redskin touchdown seemed certain.

Alas, poor Malone had to look back into a bright sun. It blinded him for a split second. Baugh's pass went right through his hands for an agonizing incompletion. The crowd groaned with disappointment. On fourth down the Redskins tried a field goal, but Bernie Masterson's kick was wide. The Bears took over on their 20, still leading 7-0.

Now Sid Luckman unveiled his new offense. It

was here that the first counter play was called. It did not go all the way for a touchdown, but the Bears could read bewilderment on the faces of the Washington linebackers. Luckman guided the Bears on a relentless, 17-play drive, never once calling a pass. He used his running backs toward the man in motion and away from the man in motion, hammering the Redskin tackles again and again.

On the 17th play of the march, Luckman, who rarely carried the ball, called a quarterback sneak and burrowed over from the one-yard-line for the touchdown. "Automatic" Jack Manders kicked the extra point and the Bears led 14-0. A few minutes later substitute Bear fullback Joe Maniaci ran 42 yards down the sideline for a third Chicago touchdown. Second-string place-kicker Phil Martinovich added the conversion and the score was 21-0.

By this time the Redskins had gotten the message. It was not to be their day. Sammy Baugh left the game and was replaced by Frank Filchock. Chicago's Ray Nolting promptly intercepted a Filchock pass on the Bear 34, and a few plays later Luckman completed a 30-yard scoring pass to Ken Kavanaugh. Halas sent in his third-string kicker, Bob Snyder, for the conversion attempt. Snyder made it to give the Bears a 28-0 half-time lead.

In the Chicago locker room coach Halas spoke to his players. "They said you were a first-half club, front-runners," he said. "Show them that you are a second-half ball club, too."

They did.

Chicago kicked off and the Redskins were

pinned far back in their own territory. On second down Sammy Baugh tried a pass into the flat. But Chicago defensive end Hampton Pool had anticipated the play. Pool slapped the ball into the air, caught it when it came down, then ran 15 yards for a touchdown. The Bears' Dick Plasman became the fourth man to make the point after touchdown and the Bears led 35-0.

Could things get worse for Washington? Amazingly, yes. Since Washington was behind by five touchdowns, Baugh risked a fourth-down pass from his own 33. But it dropped incomplete and the Bears took over. They gained ten yards on the

first play. Then Nolting went over from 23 yards out. The last man to have a chance at him was Sammy Baugh, and Nolting fooled Baugh with a fine fake. Plasman tried another extra point, but missed. Now it was "only" 41-0, Bears.

By now Sid Luckman was no longer in the game —Halas gave him the rest of the day off. The Redskins also began substituting. Since Baugh and his understudy, Filchock, had accomplished little, Washington coach Ray Flaherty tried Leroy Zimmerman at tailback. But the Bears' McAfee intercepted Zimmerman's first pass and raced 35 yards

Chicago's great George McAfee gets away from a Redskin tackler.

for his first touchdown. The fifth Bear to try an extra point, Joe Stydahar, converted to give Chicago a 48-0 lead. And before the third quarter ended, linebacker Bulldog Turner scored the Bears' eighth touchdown, returning another intercepted Zimmerman pass 21 yards. Extra point specialist number six, Joe Maniaci, had his place kick blocked as the Washington fans cheered the Redskins derisively. It was 54-0.

On the sidelines one Bear said, "This is ridiculous, beating them so bad. Let's take it easy the rest of the way." But his teammates wouldn't slow down. They remembered the names the Redskins had called them, and they continued to pour it on. The Washington players—tough, skilled professionals—were now completely disorganized and humiliated. Willie Wilkin, the Redskins' great tackle, left the game with tears of shame pouring down his face. The Redskin owner, George Preston Marshall, left the stadium in disgust during the fourth quarter. Marshall had called the Bears quitters; after this game he would decide his own players were the quitters.

The slaughter continued in the final period. On a double reverse, halfback Harry Clark sprinted 44 yards for a touchdown, the Bears' ninth. Third-string fullback Gary Famiglietti missed the extra point. Bears 60, Redskins 0.

The Redskins no sooner had the ball than disaster overtook them again. Filchock fumbled on his own two-yard-line and Chicago recovered. Chicago fullback Famiglietti quickly bucked over for the score.

This tenth Bear touchdown caused a crisis among the officials. Every time the Bears had kicked an extra point, another football had sailed into the stands—and the fans refused to give the balls back. Referee Red Friesell realized that the ball Famiglietti scored with was the only one left. Friesell went to the Chicago bench. "We're running out of footballs," he told Halas. "Would you mind running or passing for the extra point from now on?"

Halas agreed. Maniaci caught a conversion pass that made the score 67-0. The Bears scored once more on a short plunge, but this time an extra-point pass to Maniaci was incomplete. Final score: Chicago Bears 73, Washington Redskins 0.

After the game there was little the Redskin players could say. The score spoke for itself. So did the statistics. The Bears had gained 372 yards rushing to Washington's 3, and they had intercepted eight Redskin passes. But there were ironies. Washington's best runner, Farkas, had not carried the ball once during that long, bitter afternoon. "I didn't even bother to take a shower when the game was over," Andy recalls. "I just got the first plane home."

Reporters looking for the "turning point" of the game settled on the incomplete pass from Baugh to Malone in the first quarter. "Would things have been different if Malone had hung onto that ball?" one writer asked Baugh.

Sammy looked at him sorrowfully. "Yeah," he said, "the score would have been different. It would've been 73-7."

George Halas later explained the effect of the game on football strategy. "The lopsidedness of the score focused national attention on the T formation," he explained, "and when Clark Shaughnessy's Stanford team, using the same formation, ran over Nebraska in the Rose Bowl a few weeks later, the stampede to copy our offense was on."

Two years later, in 1942, the Redskins again met

the Bears for the NFL championship. This time the 'Skins were five-to-one underdogs. The Bears had won eleven straight games during the 1942 season and had recorded 18 consecutive victories in league play. But this time the psychological needle be-

The jubilant Bears leave the bench as the game ends. George Halas is at the far left.

longed to Washington's coach, Ray Flaherty. He
simply wrote the score of the 1940 game, 73-0, on
his locker room bulletin board in big, bold letters.
The Redskins could not wait to get at the Bears.
Led by Sammy Baugh, they upset the seemingly in-
vincible "Monsters of the Midway," 14-6. Thus the
Redskins got some revenge for the 1940 game, but
how could they ever really repay the Bears for in-
flicting the most spectacular defeat in pro football
history?

4.

CLEVELAND vs. PHILADELPHIA, 1950:

"We Just Met Up with a Team from the Big Leagues"

Late Saturday night, September 16, 1950, the Philadelphia Eagles emerged from their dressing room in Philadelphia's huge Municipal Stadium to meet friends and families outside. They were tired and subdued. The Eagles—defending champions of the National Football League—had just played their opening game of the season against the Cleveland Browns, who were playing their first game in the NFL. The proud Eagles had been stunned by the Browns in the first upset of the 1950s, losing 35-10.

Philadelphia's 215-pound All-NFL end, Pete Pihos, strolled into the street. His wife was there to meet him. Pihos kissed her and said quietly, "It's all right, honey. We just met up with a team from the big league."

The game was the beginning of a new NFL powerhouse—the Browns went on to dominate their division of the League for many years. But it was also the end of a long argument between two competing football leagues. Fans who remember the fierce rivalry between the American and National Football

Leagues during the 1960s will have some idea of the feeling that existed between the NFL and the All-America Conference in the late 1940s.

The All-America Conference was organized in 1946 and competed with the established NFL. But the new conference was not strong enough financially to compete for long. After the 1949 season the AAC merged with the NFL. Most of the teams went out of business, but three survived to join the NFL: the San Francisco 49ers, the Baltimore Colts and the league's perennial champions, the Cleveland Browns.

During the four years it existed, the AAC had been considered a "bush league" by NFL players and fans. The Browns had dominated the AAC. In four seasons they had played 59 league games, winning 52, losing only four and tying three. Cleveland had been beaten only once in its last 38 games. But to NFL supporters, the Browns were only "cheese champs." They had never played in the stiffer competition of the NFL.

Coached by Paul Brown, after whom the team had been named, the Browns boasted a superb passer in Otto Graham, great receivers in Mac Speedie, Dante Lavelli and Dub Jones, a booming punter in Horace Gillom, a powerful fullback in Marion Motley, a deadly place-kicker in Lou Groza, and plenty of big, fast, talented offensive and defensive players.

Coach Brown pitted this team against the veteran Eagles, who had won two NFL championships in a row and three straight Eastern Confer-

Cleveland coach Paul Brown after the Philadelphia game.

ence titles. The Eagles were coached by Greasy
Neale, whose 5-4 defensive alignment, nicknamed
the "Eagle defense," was widely used by the pros.
The key to the "Eagle defense" was a five-man line
populated by the biggest, roughest customers
coach Neale could find.

In 1950, the NFL switched to two-platoon football, and the Eagles' new defensive platoon had
some giants: linebacker Chuck Bednarik, tackles
Bucko Kilroy and "Piggy" Barnes, and All-NFL
defensive back Russ Craft. On offense they had
halfback Steve Van Buren, the NFL's biggest
ground-gainer until Jim Brown, quarterback
Tommy Thompson and end Pete Pihos.

Before the game, the tension was much like that
surrounding the 1969 Super Bowl between Baltimore of the NFL and the New York Jets of the
AFL. The Eagles and Browns knew perfectly well
that each was defending the honor of a league.
Even though the Browns were now part of the
NFL, they well remembered how the older league
and its fans had sneered at their achievements.
Cleveland wanted to prove that the AAC had been
the equal of the NFL. For their part, the Eagles
were determined not to be defeated by the upstart
"bush leaguers." They claimed they would show
the fancy-passing Brown offense what a "real"
NFL defense was like. And they would demon-
strate to the Cleveland defenders what an NFL
running attack could do.

Of the two squads, the Browns were probably
better prepared emotionally and physically. No
matter what the Philadelphia coaches said, the
Eagle players could hardly help being a little over-
confident. And the Eagle offense was handicapped
by the absence of Steve Van Buren, out with a bad
leg.

The Browns, on the other hand, were strong

physically and emotionally set for the game. As up-
starts, they were prepared to try harder. "That
game wasn't really a sporting proposition for the
Eagles," Paul Brown said later. "The press and the
public were saying how we were going to get
whipped fifty to nothing, and this would take a
little doing when we had guys like Graham, Motley, Lavelli, Speedie and Jones. This was the high-
est emotional game I ever coached. We had four
years of constant ridicule to get us ready."

Coach Brown was one of the great tacticians in
football. Like the Chicago coaching staff in 1940,
he had to detect a flaw in the defensive armor of
the opponent. He studied the famed Eagle defense
and finally found a way to pick it apart.

"In the four years we waited for this game," recalled Brown, "we gave a lot of searching thought
to the Eagle 5-4 defense. Its problem, against both
the pass and the run, was that there was no middle
linebacker. Instead there was a big, heavy middle
guard who played right in the line. So the center
was weak in the 5-4. On runs, we kept spacing our
tackles a few inches wider on each play. The Philadelphia defensive tackles would keep moving out,
too, and this created larger than usual spaces in the
Eagles' defensive line."

The Eagle linemen had been chosen more for
size and muscle than for mobility. When the
Browns made them spread farther apart than usual,
the Philadelphia middle guard became increasingly
isolated. He had to take care of running plays up
the middle without the usual shoulder-to-shoulder

support from his tackles. The wider gaps between linemen also gave the Browns' line better blocking angles. Before long they were tearing huge holes in the supposedly untearable Philadelphia line. Into those holes blasted the 240-pound Motley, one of the strongest fullbacks in NFL history. The success of the Brown running game forced the Eagles to rush quarterback Otto Graham more cautiously, giving him time to pass. Calling plays sent from the bench by coach Brown, Otto was soon picking apart the Eagle pass defense.

In the opening minute of action, the Browns went from hope to despair on one play. Halfback Don Phelps fielded an Eagle punt and sped 64 yards for a touchdown. But the Browns' blocking was a little too ardent; a Brown player was called for clipping, and the penalty nullified the touchdown. Even worse, the Cleveland kicking star, Groza, injured his shoulder on the play and was lost for the rest of the game.

But the Browns bounced back from that early disappointment. After falling behind 3-0 on a 15-yard field goal by the Eagles' Cliff Patton, Cleveland's passing circus took over, dazzling the experi-

Two Cleveland tacklers bring down Eagle ball-carrier Frank Ziegler.

enced Philadelphia defensive backs, who later confessed that they had never seen pass patterns run
with such precise timing.

From the Cleveland 41, Graham faded behind
perfect protection and spotted Dub Jones five
yards behind an Eagle defender. Graham laid the
ball right on Jones' fingertips at the Philadelphia
25, and Dub ran the rest of the way, finishing a 59-
yard scoring play. Groza's replacement, Forrest
"Chubby" Grigg, kicked the extra point, and the
Browns led 7-3.

The Cleveland defense was holding the Eagles
and soon the Browns started a touchdown drive on
their 29. Graham completed a pass to Speedie for
10 yards. He hit Motley on a flare pattern, and
Marion rumbled for 20 yards. Then Otto hit Jones
for seven yards, bringing the ball to the Eagle 34.
The Philadelphia defense was now thoroughly
pass-conscious, so Paul Brown shuttled in a running play. Motley burst through the weakly de-
fended middle on a trap play to the Eagle 26. Now
Brown and Graham used their star receiver, Dante
Lavelli, for the first time since early in the first
quarter. Lavelli got clear over the middle and
caught Graham's accurate spiral right between the
goal posts. The extra point was good and Cleveland
led 14-3.

At half time the Eagles tried to regroup and ad-
just their defense. But it was no use. Philadelphia
was not fully prepared to react to what the Browns
were doing. The Eagles' tinkering during the half-
time intermission was too little and too late.

The Browns' receiver Mac Speedie looks for the goal after catching a pass from Otto Graham.

The Browns took the second-half kickoff. Graham completed five straight passes, bringing the ball to the Eagle 12. After an incompletion he squirmed out of the grasp of Eagle lineman Norm "Wild Man" Willey, and fired a scoring pass to Speedie. Grigg's place kick made the score 21-3. The Browns had broken the game wide open.

The Eagles scored next, going over on a 17-yard

pass to Pete Pihos. But when Cleveland got the ball
back it switched to its power running game and
continued to dominate play. Too widely spaced,
thanks to Paul Brown's planning, the frustrated
Eagle linemen kept giving ground. In the remaining
time, the Browns scored twice more to make the
game a runaway. The final score was 35-10.

In 1946, when the old AAC was organized,
Elmer Layden, the NFL commissioner, said: "Let
them get a football." The Browns had gotten a
football, and four years later they were teaching the
NFL how to use it. Their running game had caught
up with the Eagle defense, but it was the passing of
Otto Graham that finished the Eagles. Graham attempted 38 passes and completed 21 for a total of
346 yards and three touchdowns. The Brown
offense had prospered against a defense considered
much too strong for the "cheese champs" of a de-
funct "bush league."

The Browns-Eagles game had been advertised as
"the most talked-about game in NFL history." It
was widely discussed, all right, but not in the way
the experts had expected. The conversation now
centered on the beautifully organized Browns—
and their remarkable coach, Paul Brown. "They've
got a lot of guns," said Greasy Neale after the
game. "They're a good football team." Then the
Eagle coach reconsidered and corrected himself.
"They're a *very* fine football team."

Paul Brown's demonstration of power against
the Eagles also put an end to the Eagle defense
with its five-man line and cumbersome middle

The Cleveland hero, Otto Graham, receives a trophy as Best Player after the game.

guard. The new trend was toward a four-man defensive line supported by three linebackers, including an agile middle linebacker. This 4-3 defense is
still standard in pro football.

In 1950 the Browns went on to win the NFL
championship. In the championship game they
edged the Los Angeles Rams 30-28 when Lou
Groza kicked a field goal in the final minute of
play. But the best-remembered game of the season
was that first shocking confrontation between the
Browns and the defending NFL champs.

As Eagle Pete Pihos told his wife, the proud
Eagles "met up with a team from the big league."

5.

DETROIT vs. SAN FRANCISCO, 1957:
"The Bomb" Explodes

During the year 1957 two things were put in the air. One was called Sputnik I, the historic space capsule in which Soviet cosmonaut Yuri Gagarin became the first man to orbit the earth. Closer to the ground, on the playing fields of the National Football League, the San Francisco 49ers had their own version of Sputnik and Gagarin. His name was R. C. Owens. He played wide receiver for the 49ers with a flamboyance few receivers have equaled before or since.

The six-foot, three-inch Owens was famous for a unique play called the "Alley-Oop." It went this way: R.C. would run a deep pattern into the enemy end zone. Then San Francisco quarterback Y. A. Tittle would loft a high, arching pass in Owens' general direction. The idea was that ball, Owens and his defender would arrive at the same spot at the same time. Owens had tremendous spring in his legs. He didn't quite go into orbit, but he reportedly *could* jump six feet into the air. R.C. usually outleaped the man guarding him and came down with the football—and a touchdown. Some rivals called the "Alley-Oop" play just a show-business gimmick, but nobody could deny its success.

In 1957 the 49ers finished in a tie with the Detroit Lions for the Western Division title. In addition to the "Alley-Oop," they had an outstanding passer in Y. A. Tittle, sometimes called the "Bald Eagle." They also had one of the greatest running

combinations in the game, the powerful Joe Perry
for inside and Hugh "The King" McElhenny outside. All-Pro offensive tackle Bob St. Clair, who
stood 6-foot-9 and weighed 265 pounds, looked
more like a basketball center, but he was a fero-

The 49ers' "Alley-Oop" man, R. C. Owens, leaps high (left) and grabs the
ball (above).

cious tackler and he shocked his NFL colleagues by eating raw meat.

This great San Francisco team, coached by Frankie Albert, had compiled an 8-4 regular-season record. (Albert had been the 49ers' regular quarterback and, before that, had been football's first classic T-formation quarterback. A few weeks after the Chicago Bears routed the Redskins 73-0 with the T formation, Frankie Albert quarterbacked Stanford to a similar T-formation victory over the University of Alabama in the 1941 Rose Bowl.)

San Francisco's great offensive unit was to face a great Detroit Lion defensive team in the game to decide the Western Division winner. There was nothing wrong with the Lion offense when it was healthy. But as the team went into this crucial game, the offense was not healthy—and had not been since early in the season, when first-string quarterback Bobby Layne broke his leg. Fortunately, Detroit had acquired quarterback Tobin Rote from Green Bay, and Rote had done an excellent job. Tobin was not a dropback pocket passer. At 6-foot-3 and 220 pounds, he was a rambunctious rollout quarterback who liked to carry the football almost as much as he liked to throw it.

But Detroit's pride was its defense, particularly its defensive secondary, nicknamed "Chris' Crew" after its leader, Jack Christiansen. The rest of the crew were Yale Lary, the extremely hard-nosed Jim David, and Carl Karilivacz. They were justifiably celebrated for their skillful use of the zone pass defense—and.their ability to shut off the deep pass. Since the nub of the 49ers' air game was the deep pass, the experts expected an epic confrontation: pass offense against pass defense.

The battle for the West was fought on the 49ers' home turf, Kezar Stadium in San Francisco, before a full-house crowd of 60,000 people. Despite superb personnel the 49ers had trouble winning big games. During their existence in the old All-America Conference, they had never been able to defeat the Cleveland Browns for the league championship. And since entering the NFL in 1950, they had never won even a divisional title. But 1957 seemed to be the year.

San Francisco had another emotional force powering it. In October, while watching his team play the Chicago Bears at Kezar, 49er founder and owner Tony Morabito had collapsed and died of a heart attack. Morabito had been very generous to his players and was popular with them. When the players were told of Morabito's death at the half, they were trailing 17-7. They went back on the field, overtook the Bears, won the game 21-17— and played like demons the remainder of the year. They had vowed to win this Western playoff game for Morabito.

For the first 30 minutes it seemed as if the keyed-up 49ers would run the Lions into San Francisco Bay. Early in the game punter Bill Jessup of the 49ers pinned Detroit deep in its own territory with a kick that went out of bounds on the Lion nine-yard-line. Seconds later, Detroit's rookie fullback,

John Henry Johnson, was hit hard and fumbled. San Francisco recovered on the Detroit 21. A penalty pushed the ball back to the 35, but the 49ers would not be stopped. Tittle opened with a screen pass that fell incomplete. Then he called his first "Alley-Oop" play of the day.

R. C. Owens raced down the field and Tittle looped his usual rainbow pass in his direction. R.C. outleaped defender Jim David on the goal line and fell into the end zone for six points. Gordy Soltau converted to give San Francisco a 7-0 lead.

After taking the kickoff, the Lions ran three inconclusive plays, then punted to the San Francisco 41. It took Tittle only three plays to cover the 59 yards to the Detroit end zone. The score came on a 47-yard pass play from Y.A. to running back Hugh McElhenny. Soltau's place kick made it San Francisco 14, Detroit 0.

Now the Lions showed their teeth, driving 61 yards for a touchdown in eight plays, including key completions to ends Dave Middleton, Jim Doran, then Middleton again. With the ball on the San Francisco 7, Rote kept passing—but the 49er defense stiffened and two straight passes fell incomplete in the end zone. On third down halfback Howard "Hopalong" Cassady hit the line for three yards. On fourth down, disdaining to attempt a field goal, Rote faded to pass. He found the redheaded rookie tight end, Steve Junker, in the clear and threw Junker a four-yard touchdown pass. "Jungle Jim" Martin's extra point made the score 49ers 14, Lions 7.

Undaunted, the 49ers continued to press. Tittle
was known as a gambling, free-passing quarterback, but now he guided his team on a highly disci-
plined 19-play march. For the most part, Tittle
called running plays. But three times, in third-and-
long-yardage situations, he found end Billy Wilson
for vital, first-down completions. Finally Tittle

San Francisco end Billy Wilson makes a catch. The Lion defender is Jack
Christiansen, who later was the 49ers' coach.

passed to Wilson in the end zone, and Billy made a glorious leaping catch. Soltau's extra point raised the 49er lead to 21-7.

A few minutes later the 49ers got possession of the ball by recovering a fumble on the Lion 41. They drove into field goal range and Gordie Soltau kicked a three-pointer to make the score 24-7.

Able to move the ball against the formidable Detroit defense, and able to stop the Lion offense, the 49ers had a 17-point lead and seemed in command of the day. It was at this juncture, however, that Uncle Upset appeared. For this was to be a Sunday on which two separate football games would be played in Kezar Stadium. The 49ers had won the first half. Now it was the Detroit Lions' turn.

As the second half began, the 49ers picked up where they had left off. Receiving the kickoff, they strong-armed their way toward Lion territory. Then Tittle gave the ball to McElhenny, who danced his way down, down, down the field, evading Lion tacklers until he was finally knocked down on the Detroit 2. Another San Francisco touchdown seemed inevitable. It would give the 49ers an insurmountable 31-7 lead.

But San Francisco never got that clinching touchdown. Three times the 49er runners slammed into the Detroit line—and three times the Lions threw them back. On fourth down Soltau kicked a 12-yard field goal to give his team a 27-7 lead. It still looked bad for the Lions, but they had received an important psychological lift from their goal-line stand. Nobody knew it then, but the San Francisco

49ers had scored their last points of the game—and
of the year.

Mistakes had cost Detroit dearly in the first half.
Now it was San Francisco's turn to stumble. Tittle
fumbled on his 27-yard-line, and Bob Long of the
Lions landed on the football. You could see re-
newed life blossom all along the Detroit bench.
Maybe the game wasn't over yet . . .

It wasn't. Off that Detroit bench came second-
string fullback Tom Tracy. A stocky, 205-pound
runner, Tracy was neither overwhelmingly powerful nor extremely fast. But he was a fighter, and his
ability to squirt through small holes for big yardage
had earned him the nickname of "Tom the Bomb."
With Detroit's regular backs hobbled by injuries,
coach George Wilson sent "The Bomb" in, hoping
for an explosion. He got one. Nine plays later
Tracy slashed over for a touchdown from the San
Francisco one-yard-line. Martin converted and
now the 49ers led by "only" 27-14.

With fresh determination the Lion defense dug
in and stopped the 49ers cold. San Francisco's Jessup punted to the Detroit 41. After one play gained
a yard, Tobin Rote sent Tom Tracy off right tackle.
There wasn't much of a hole, but "The Bomb"
wriggled through it, cut back behind a wall of
blockers and chugged 58 yards into the San Francisco end zone. The 49ers were almost as shocked
as their silent fans. A huge San Francisco lineman
had apparently stopped Tracy at the line of scrimmage, only to see him slip away. Jim Martin's
fourth extra point made it 49ers 27, Lions 21. The

two Detroit touchdowns had come 61 seconds apart. It was enough to demoralize the 49ers—and it did.

Again San Francisco tried to move the football —and again Detroit forced a punt. Taking over on their 46, the Lions scored in five plays, with Gene Gedman plunging the final two yards. Martin's point-after kick put the Lions ahead for the first time, 28-27. The clock told the story in two ways. First, it revealed that the Lions had overtaken the 49ers with awesome speed, packing three touchdowns and 21 points into one minute and 47 seconds of playing time. Second, it showed that Detroit nosed ahead with only one minute gone in the fourth quarter. The explosive 49ers had 14 minutes —plenty of time—in which to catch up.

Now the tone of the game changed. Where it had been wide open and high scoring, now it became tense and conservative. The momentum still seemed to be with the Lions. Joe Perry of the 49ers fumbled and tackle Gil Mains of Detroit recovered. But now the San Francisco defense rose up and prevented a score. Then Carl Karilivacz of Detroit intercepted a Tittle pass to give his team another scoring chance. The Lions plowed right to the edge of the end zone. But then, as he struggled to inch across, hero Tom Tracy lost the football and the 49ers recovered.

Desperately, Tittle returned to his passing game.

Stocky Tom Tracy, Detroit's "bomb," chugs into the end zone for a touchdown.

He had had time to pick his receivers in the first
half, during which he had completed 12 of 19
passes. But in the disastrous second half, Y.A. was
given a hard rush and his receivers were closely
covered by "Chris' Crew." Tittle completed 6 of 12
passes in the second half, but he was intercepted
three times. The second interception came shortly

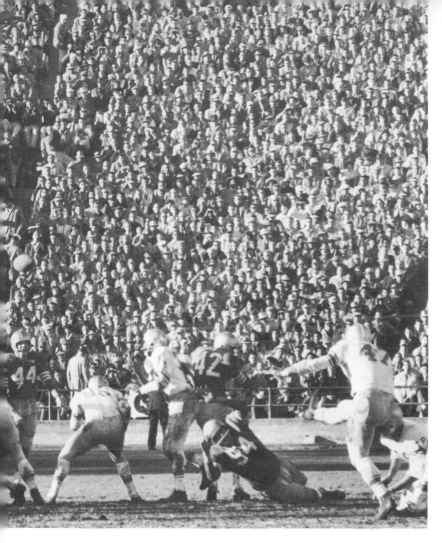

Detroit's Jim Martin kicks the field goal that clinched the Lions' upset victory.

after the 49ers had grabbed Tracy's fumble inside the one-yard-line. Middle linebacker Joe Schmidt picked off a Tittle pass. Jim Martin kicked a 13-yard field goal for Detroit, and the score was Detroit 31, San Francisco 27.

A few moments later the game ended. As the

49ers filed off the field in the dusk, they could not quite believe what had happened to them. The following season, 1958, coach Albert benched Tittle and began to rely more and more on young quarterback John Brodie. Albert himself came under fire for benching Tittle, and resigned just before the final game of the 1958 season. Tittle stayed with the 49ers through 1960. Then San Francisco virtually gave him to the New York Giants where Tittle had a "second childhood," again becoming a top-flight, record-setting quarterback.

There also was a fascinating irony on the Lion side of the field. One of Detroit's stars, Jack Christiansen, later achieved fame in the uniform of the 49ers, serving as San Francisco's head coach from 1963 through 1966.

The drama of the Lions' comeback-upset made Detroit's NFL championship game against the Eastern Division champion Cleveland Browns almost an anticlimax. The Browns had humiliated the Lions by a 56-10 score for the 1954 league championship. Now the Lions returned the compliment. In 1957 they crushed Cleveland 59-14, completing a dramatic and victorious season.

6.

DETROIT vs. GREEN BAY, 1962:
The Turkey Day Massacre

It was the kind of call that turns coaches gray and causes quarterbacks to be traded. In the fourth game of the 1962 season the Detroit Lions led the Green Bay Packers 7-6. With less than two minutes to play, the Lions had the ball and were killing the clock. They clicked off two first downs, but then the Packer defense braced. Two running plays gained little ground, making it third and eight.

Lion quarterback Milt Plum conferred with his coach, George Wilson, on the sideline, then returned to the huddle. The conservative, safe call was a running play. The run would probably not pick up the first down, but it would use up more valuable time. Then the Lions could punt and the Packers would have to cover about 70 yards in about 30 seconds to win. Almost everybody expected the Lions to run.

But on instructions from the coach, Milt Plum did not make the safe, conservative call. Instead he called an unexpected pass. Receiver Terry Barr slanted toward the middle of the field, then sud-

denly cut toward the sideline. But as Plum threw,
tragedy tripped the Lions. Barr slipped and fell.
Plum's pass zipped right to where Barr should have
been. But standing there instead was Packer cornerback Herb Adderley, who intercepted the pass
and returned it 30 yards. With 33 seconds to go in
the game, Green Bay's Paul Hornung kicked his
third field goal of the day and the Packers won 9-7.
Detroit had blown its chance for a big upset win.

In the plane on the way back to Detroit, some
Lion players complained bitterly about the pass
play that had lost the game. "We should have run,"
they said. "We should have run."

Suddenly coach Wilson's voice came over the
plane's intercom. "That was a tough one out there
today," he said. "No one hates to lose more than I
do. But remember this: the mark of great teams is
that they are able to come back. You can't bring
that game back, so forget it. But just get one thing
straight. I called that play. Nobody else did. I still
think we have the best team in our division and the
best quarterback. And we *will* win this thing."

Coach Wilson was proved wrong in some respects. The standings at season's end showed that
he did not have the best team in the NFL West, nor
the best quarterback. But out of the ashes of that
heartbreaking defeat in Green Bay came one of the
classic upsets in NFL history.

Late in the 1962 season the Lions played the
Packers again in their traditional Thanksgiving
Day game. By that time Green Bay was being
called the greatest football team of all time. "The

Pack" had won eleven straight league games and had not been beaten in 19 games. An undefeated year seemed almost certain for coach Vince Lombardi's Big Green Machine.

But that was before Thanksgiving. After the game, the Packers were simply thankful to get out of Detroit's Tiger Stadium alive. The Lions, striking furiously from the start, virtually flawless on offense and defense, shattered the Packers 26-14. And the game was not as close as the final score indicates. The Lions did more than win; they gave the Packers a ferocious physical beating—probably the worst whipping a Lombardi-coached team ever received.

In particular, the Detroit defense turned Green Bay's All-Pro quarterback, Bart Starr, into a Thanksgiving turkey. The Lions did everything but stuff Starr and pick his wishbone apart. Tackles Alex Karras and Roger Brown and ends Sam Williams and Darris McCord were Detroit's principal attackers. The Packers supposedly had the finest offensive line in the league, but the Lions' defensive line stormed in on Starr again and again, brushing aside the famous Green Bay blocking guards, Jerry Kramer and Fuzzy Thurston, with ease. The Lion linebackers—Wayne Walker, Joe Schmidt and Carl Brettschneider—helped out, too. In the first half alone, the Lions sacked Starr eight times for losses totaling 76 yards.

As he found himself buried with increasing frequency under 1,000 pounds of gristle in blue jerseys, Starr became more and more angry. Bart was normally a perfect gentleman on and off the field, but this time it was more than he could take.

"Those big Lion linemen kept knocking me down like a bowling pin," he recalled years later, "and I got madder and madder. With a minute to go, I got to the point where I began to blame the officials for our defeat. I was standing on the sidelines when Red Paice, the referee, trotted by.

" 'Hey, ref,' I shouted, 'if you give us any more of those lousy calls, I'm going to reach out and bite that big, fat head of yours right off!'

"Paice stared right into my face and told me, 'Starr, if you do, you'll be the only quarterback in this league with more brains in his stomach than he has in his head!' "

Starr grinned wryly as he retold the story. "It was the perfect squelch," he admitted, "and I knew I had it coming."

But it took more than an overpowering pass rush to stop the Packer attack. A sly but significant change in tactics by the Detroit defensive secondary had a lot to do with it, too. Lion safetyman Dick "Night Train" Lane explained the change to author-illustrator Robert Riger. Usually, he said, the pass defenders shift to the strong side—the side where the offensive team positions its wide receiver. But the Lion defenders crossed up the Packers by doubling up on receiver Max McGee even when he was the end on the weak side.

"We kept Wayne Walker in front of him and Dick LeBeau behind him as he ran his patterns," Lane continued, "so that Bart couldn't get the

On three different plays, Packer quarterback Bart Starr tries to escape Lion tacklers (above), gets jumped on (below), and is dragged to the ground (following pages).

quick pass off to Max. Starr had to hold up the pass and the line hit him for those losses."

Some reporters asked Vince Lombardi after the game why the Packers hadn't tried screen passes, a common way to slow down the pass rush. On a screen, the quarterback waits until the pass rushers have committed themselves, then flips the pass over their heads. One or two successful screen passes often slow down the pass rush.

"Starr can't work the screen," Lombardi replied honestly. "I don't know what it is. It takes a certain kind of quarterback to make it work. Bart can do a great many things, but that's not one of them."

Detroit's right tackle Brown was the pass rush hero. He was a 303-pound lineman with speed that had to be seen to be believed. In training camp, Roger had raced blazing-fast track star Glenn Davis in a 25-yard dash. Davis had won gold medals in the longer dashes at the 1956 and 1960 Olympics, but Roger Brown nipped him by a step at 25 yards—and barely lost at 50 yards.

Bart Starr later confessed, "I've never been rushed like that in my life." Brown said, "I guess I got to know Bart pretty well out there today."

Vince Lombardi knew what had happened. "They were getting a jump on us something awful," he said after it was all over. "We adjusted some during the first half, but not enough. The Lions made a quick charge on every play in the first half. We weren't ready for it. It wasn't that our offensive line had a bad day. I've just never seen a defensive line come off as fast as the Lions did."

While the Detroit defense justifiably received credit for breaking the game open, actually it was two brilliant passes from Milt Plum to end Gail Cogdill that gave the Lions the lead they never lost.

In the first quarter, the Lions were on the Green Bay 34 with third down and four yards to go. The Packers were expecting a short pass, but Plum crossed them up. Gail Cogdill went speeding down the left sideline with defender Herb Adderley playing him tight to prevent the quick short pass.

The Lions' Gail Cogdill makes one of his two touchdown catches in the end zone.

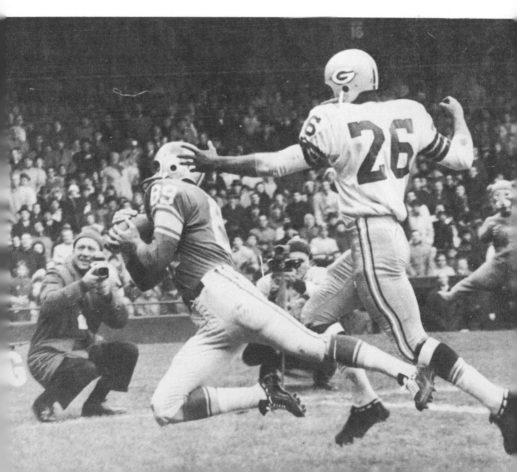

Cogdill got behind Adderley, raced all the way downfield, and made a glittering fingertip catch in the end zone.

The score held at 7-0, Lions, until the Plum-to-Cogdill combination connected again in the second quarter. Plum lofted the ball right where Cogdill could catch it near the back line of the end zone.

"The pass was supposed to go to halfback Tommy Watkins," Cogdill explained. "I told Milt to throw one in the corner of the end zone if Watkins was covered. I was looking Adderley right in the eye. I knew that if I stuck up my hands he'd know the ball was coming. So I delayed as long as I could, then grabbed the pass at the last second."

Now the Lions were leading 14-0. The Packers fumbled the kickoff and were pinned deep in their own territory. On third down with long yardage, Starr tried to complete a pass to pull his team out of the hole. He searched frantically for a free receiver, but all he found was the muscular embrace of big Roger Brown. The Detroit lineman hit Starr so hard that the ball squirted loose. Defensive end Sam Williams scooped it up on the Packer six and lumbered over the goal line to give Detroit a three-touchdown lead.

On the next set of downs, Brown cracked down again. This time he caught Starr in the Packer end zone, scoring a safety. This put Detroit ahead 23-0.

Just before the first half ended, the Packers organized their first real drive. They reached the Lion 26, but then the Detroit defense held. On fourth down, Jerry Kramer, filling in for the injured Paul

Hornung, attempted a field goal. The kick went wide and a few minutes later the half was over.

The Lions had had a spectacular half against football's "greatest team." Not only had they caught Starr eight times, they had shut off Green Bay's great fullback, Jim Taylor. Taylor gained three yards on eight first-half carries.

Early in the second half the Lions had one more roar. "Night Train" Lane intercepted a Starr pass at the Detroit 42. Then Milt Plum, playing the

Detroit quarterback Milt Plum hands off to a running back.

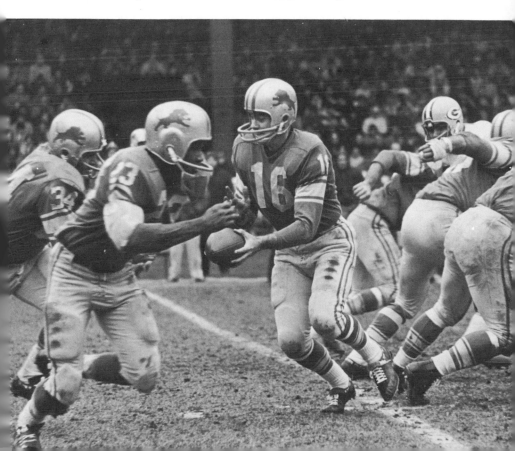

game of his life, kicked a 47-yard field goal.

With the Lions leading 26-0, the Packers rallied to make the score look respectable. Their first touchdown came on a freak play. With the ball on his 28, Plum went back to pass, but somehow the toss wound up in the hands of Green Bay defensive end Bill Quinlan. Quinlan was so startled that he promptly fumbled the ball. The other Packer end, Willie Davis, recovered the ball in the end zone for a touchdown. The play did not affect the outcome of the game, but it irritated Detroit's assistant coach, Scooter McLean. He wanted to shut the Packers out "just so we could say they hadn't gotten a touchdown on us all year."

Green Bay had one last shot. With six minutes to play, Lion fullback Ken Webb, in for the injured Nick Pietrosante, fumbled on his own 14. Again Willie Davis fell on the ball. A few plays later Jim Taylor sliced over from the four to give the Packers their second score. Amazingly, the potent Green Bay offense couldn't claim much credit for a single score. One touchdown was made by a defensive player and the second was made after a drive of only 14 yards.

The victory put the Lions only one game behind the Packers in the Western Division standings. If only they had held on to the lead in that earlier game, they would have been tied with the Packers. The Packers recovered from their Thanksgiving Day humiliation, however, and went on to win both the division and league championships.

The Lions could be proud of that game, however. They had broken Green Bay's long winning streak and proved that the Green Bay machine could be beaten. The defeat was one of the worst in Green Bay's history—for one day, the Lions had turned Vince Lombardi's "run to daylight" dream into a nightmare.

7.

CLEVELAND vs. BALTIMORE, 1964:
"They Told Us This Was a Lousy Team"

In the years since 1950 two of the NFL's most consistently successful teams have been the Baltimore Colts and the Cleveland Browns. The Colts were led for many of those years by the game's top quarterback, Johnny Unitas. The Browns were first masterminded by coach Paul Brown and quarterback Otto Graham, then sparked by fullback Jim Brown, the finest running back of modern times.

Yet, curiously, in championship-game competition, the Colts and Browns were erratic. Both were like the little girl in the nursery rhyme—when they were good, they were very, very good, and when they were bad, they were horrid.

The Browns started out strong, entering the league in 1950 with their upset of the Eagles, and then defeating Los Angeles for the title. But in 1954 they were humiliated 56-10 in the championship game by Detroit. More recently, they were whipped 54-14 by the Cowboys in a 1967 conference title game and 34-0 by the Colts in the 1968 NFL championship. They came back in 1969 to beat the Cowboys 38-14 for the Eastern title, but lost the very next week in the championship game 27-7, to the Vikings.

The Colts? They were very, very good against the Giants in 1958, winning a historic sudden-death overtime game 23-17. They were even better in 1959, walloping the Giants 31-16 for their second consecutive NFL title. But in 1969 the Colts entered the Super Bowl as solid favorites against the Jets—and lost 16-7. Then in the 1970 Super Bowl, they hung on to beat Dallas. But the very next year, when they were fully expected to reach the Super Bowl to defend their title, the Colts tripped embarrassingly. The Miami Dolphins shut them out and humiliated them in the AFC championship game.

And then there was 1964.

In 1964 the up-and-down Colts and Browns met for the championship. This time nearly everything favored the Colts. Led by Johnny Unitas, they had had the highest-scoring offense in the league, and the Colt defense had given up the fewest points. Cleveland had done nearly as well on offense, but the defense had given up 68 more points than the Colt defense. Although they had won their conference title, the Browns were not taken very seriously. They were seven-point underdogs going into the game, even though they were playing at home. Many experts expected the game to be more lopsided. The rugged Baltimore defense would contain, if not stop, rushing champion Jim Brown, said the experts, while Unitas would make hash of the doubtful Cleveland defense.

It did not happen that way at all. In one of the most shattering, yet overlooked, upsets in NFL annals, the Browns rose up and gave the Colts a terrific 27-0 beating, overpowering them in every phase of the game. In winning their first league title since 1955, the Browns shut out the Colts for the first time in 31 games. "I saw it, but I don't believe it," said one Baltimore executive.

The Cleveland offense was outstanding. But the key to the game was the frequently ridiculed Cleveland defense.

"All year long," said Blanton Collier, the Cleveland head coach, "our defensive team has been maligned and kicked around, and I think they were just determined to come up with a great effort in the championship game."

Two of the three elements of the Cleveland defense were considered questionable. The linebackers were all right, but the defensive backs (Bernie Parrish, Walter Beach, Ross Fichtner and Larry Benz) were considered too small; all stood less than six feet tall.

The Browns' front four—ends Paul Wiggin and Bill Glass, tackles Dick Modzelewski and Jim Kanicki—were hardly famous for a hard, fast pass rush. Yet in order to win, the Cleveland defensive line would have to rush Unitas. Give him enough time to find his receivers and you would give him the game. One particular mismatch seemed to be Cleveland's second-year, 250-pound defensive tackle Kanicki against Baltimore's 270-pound All-Pro guard, Jim Parker. Parker was expected to eat Kanicki alive.

Cleveland's game plan was simple. "First we went back to fundamentals," said coach Collier. Given two weeks to prepare for the Colts, Collier devoted one of them to the rudiments of blocking and tackling. Only then did he and his staff consider the Colts themselves.

"We decided," Collier explained, "that we wanted to have everybody covered when Unitas took his first look at his primary receiver. That way

The underrated Cleveland defensive line—Jim Kanicki (69), Bill Glass (80) and Dick Modzelewski (background)—pull down Colt quarterback Johnny Unitas.

he'd have to look for a second receiver. And if he still didn't see anyone open, maybe he'd wait some more. By then our pass rush should be on him. But there's nothing startling about that."

Making plans to cover the fast, smart Baltimore receivers was one thing; covering them in a game was something else. The Browns got some help by making a tactical change that surprised and finally defeated the Colts.

"We've been known as a team that plays receivers very loose," said Bernie Parrish, the on-field brains of the Cleveland secondary. "We've given receivers the short yardage. I feel that the Colts expected us to back off and play them loose. I thought we'd do better by playing their receivers close. So did our coaches."

As a result, Parrish practically played inside Jimmy Orr's jersey, and Beach clung tightly to Raymond Berry. When assistance was required, it came from safetymen Benz and Fichtner. "We moved up and crowded their receivers, forcing them to cut before they wanted to," Fichtner said.

Thus when Unitas looked for an open man, he rarely found one. Six times during the game Unitas raised his arm to pass, couldn't locate a free receiver, and had to pull the football down and run with it. He gained yardage, but as Cleveland defensive lineman Bill Glass put it, "I'd rather see him run than pass."

And it wasn't only the Cleveland secondary that won its battle against the Baltimore offense. The Browns' defensive line did the unexpected and outmuscled the Colt blockers. They took away the Baltimore running game and punched big holes in Unitas' pass protection. In particular, Kanicki had a glorious day against Parker, who could not seem to stop the aggressive young Cleveland lineman. Time and again Kanicki would apply such a fierce inside rush that Unitas' pass pocket would literally be hurled back into his face. And with the front four penetrating so well, the Cleveland linebackers were able to drop back on pass plays, clogging the receivers' lanes. Wherever Unitas looked, he saw Cleveland shirts.

The game started slowly, with no scoring in the first half. But it was soon clear that the Baltimore offense was experiencing problems with the Cleveland defense. The Colts' deepest penetration of the half came early in the second quarter when they reached the Browns' 19 after a pass interception. But when Lou Michaels tried a fourth-down field goal, holder Bob Boyd fumbled the snap from center and the Browns took over.

Cleveland emphasized its running game at first, seeking to make the Colts aware of it in order to open the passing zones. The Browns had one good scoring chance, but rookie receiver Paul Warfield slipped while running a pass route on the Colts' 10 and the pass was caught instead by Baltimore linebacker Don Shinnick.

Despite the scoreless tie at half time, the Browns had accomplished much. Their defense was throwing the famous Colts back, and the Browns had established their ground game. And Cleveland had

observed that the Colts were repeatedly giving
Warfield double coverage while allowing Gary Col-
lins to be taken one-on-one by cornerback Boyd.
They could take advantage of that latter matchup.

As the second half began, the Browns had a
powerful ally: a 20-mile-per-hour wind at their
backs. The first time they had the ball, the Colts
had to punt into that wind. Tom Gilburg's kick carried only 25 yards, setting up a Browns' field goal
by Lou Groza. That put Cleveland ahead 3-0.

Most of the 79,544 fans in Municipal Stadium
expected that score to sting the Colts into action.
Even the most rabid Cleveland fans wondered if
the Browns' "rubber band defense" could stop Baltimore for 60 minutes. But there was no sign of
weakening. Again the defense forced the Colts to
punt into the wind. This time Gilburg's short punt
rolled dead on the Cleveland 32.

On first down Jim Brown gained four yards. On
second down Cleveland lined up in an unusual
double wing formation. Only Brown lined up behind quarterback Frank Ryan. Ryan pitched out to
Jim, who followed three blockers around the left
side, turned the corner, then cut back toward
midfield and rumbled 46 yards to the Baltimore 18.
From there Ryan wasted no time. He hit Collins
with an 18-yard touchdown pass. Groza converted
and it was Cleveland 10, Colts 0.

Later, Ryan said that his call on this first touchdown pass to Collins was the most important decision he had to make all afternoon.

"We had established tremendous momentum,"

Above, Cleveland quarterback Frank Ryan throws. Below, receiver Gary Collins makes one of his three touchdown receptions.

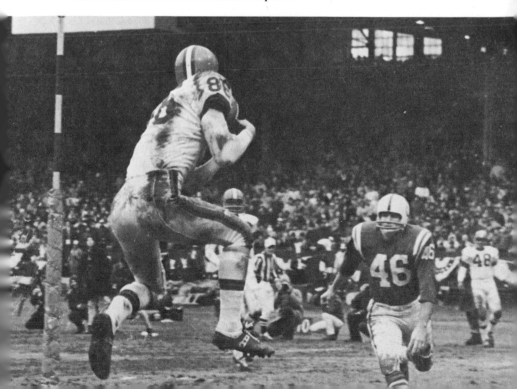

he said. "The running was going; we had just gained 46 yards on a running play, and I was tempted to call another sweep. But maybe the defense would call an outside blitz and they would drop Jim for a long loss. Then I thought, maybe we can go inside. But if they cut off the inside, we wouldn't gain and the momentum would go from us to them. I knew they had been playing Collins for a hook pass all afternoon. I decided to call a hook-and-go to Gary, on which he does a hook, then breaks downfield. He was wide open between the goal posts."

According to Baltimore cornerback Boyd, Collins was wide open because the Colts missed their defensive signals. "We couldn't hear our calls because of the crowd noise," Boyd said, explaining rather than excusing. "We blew one on that play and we blew another one later. The guy who was supposed to take the middle deep took the outside instead."

The other mistake Boyd referred to happened a few minutes later. This time the great Baltimore defensive back Jerry Logan misread a Cleveland formation. Instead of covering the deep middle zone, Logan went elsewhere. Collins raced into the vacant area and made a beautiful catch of Ryan's long lead pass for a 42-yard touchdown play. Groza's kick made it 17-0.

In the fourth quarter the Browns faced the fierce wind themselves, but it didn't seem to slow them down. Jim Brown smashed for 21 yards, and two

The great Jimmy Brown plows through Colt tacklers.

pass completions, one to Warfield and one to tight end Johnny Brewer, put the ball on the Colts' one-yard-line. Frantically, Baltimore dug in and threw Brown back on three line plunges. But on fourth down Groza kicked an easy field goal to make it 20-0, Cleveland.

Even at this point a Colt comeback did not seem impossible. Unitas was a wizard at making comeback drives. But the Cleveland defense wouldn't let go. Again the Browns took possession. Now Ryan gambled. He guessed that the Colts would expect him to play a conservative running game and use up the clock. Instead, he put the ball in the air, long and high. Collins ran under it, made a fantastic catch and went over for his third touchdown. The play covered 51 yards. Groza made the point-after kick and the Browns led 27-0.

The statistics, which often can lie, told the story of this game quite accurately. The Colts never did score and they got inside the Brown 20-yard-line only once. Cleveland's defense held Baltimore's offense to 82 yards rushing and 89 passing. Unitas, who had thrown only six interceptions all year, had two passes picked off by Cleveland's middle linebacker Vince Costello. The Browns, on the other hand, gained 142 yards rushing and 197 passing. Collins had five receptions for 130 yards and three touchdowns, and received the Most Valuable Player award. Jim Brown had run for 124 yards in 27 carries.

One writer, who had seen every Brown game since 1946, called this game "their best performance ever." And the Cleveland players could not help but crow a little.

"You can't possibly know how great it feels," said center John Morrow. "It's especially great because everybody kept telling us how the Colts couldn't be beat."

Reporters surrounded big Jim Brown in the locker room. A year later the great back would retire from football, but in 1964 Brown was football's top player. He was a blunt, honest man who could not make himself seem more excited than he was. Said Brown that day, "This is the finest feeling I have ever had."

Quarterback Ryan, who completed 11 of 18 passes, praised the forgotten offensive linemen who had kept the Colt rushers away from him and had pried open holes for the Cleveland backs. "If Art Modell [the team's owner] won't give the offensive linemen a raise next year, then Jim Brown and I will," Ryan said.

Also not to be forgotten was the defensive unit. The "rubber band defense" had shut out the mighty Colts. Jim Kanicki, thought to be the weakest link, was one of the stars. The Browns had excelled at everything. On this day they were the team that was "very, very good."

After the game, Buddy Young, a Colts executive, walked into the Cleveland dressing room to congratulate the winners. Young could not hide his disbelief. "They told us this was a lousy team," he said with a hollow laugh. "They sure told us wrong."

8.

GREEN BAY vs. DALLAS, 1967:
A Starr Shines at 13 Below

Great white clouds of steam billowed from the mouths of the white-shirted, silver-helmeted Dallas Cowboys as they lined up to receive the kickoff. It was early in the second period and the Green Bay Packers had just scored their second touchdown to take a 14-0 lead.

It was December 1967. The Cowboys and the Packers were playing for the NFL championship in Green Bay under the worst weather conditions imaginable. The temperature was 13 degrees below zero, but the chill factor (which also takes wind and humidity into account) made it feel like 38 below. The day was more suited to polar bears and penguins than passes and punts. It was particularly hard on the Dallas players, who trained and played most of their games in warmer climates.

The Packers, who were seeking their third NFL championship in a row, had taken charge early. They marched to a touchdown the first time they got their hands on the ball, tramping 82 yards in 16 plays. Receiver Boyd Dowler caught Bart Starr's

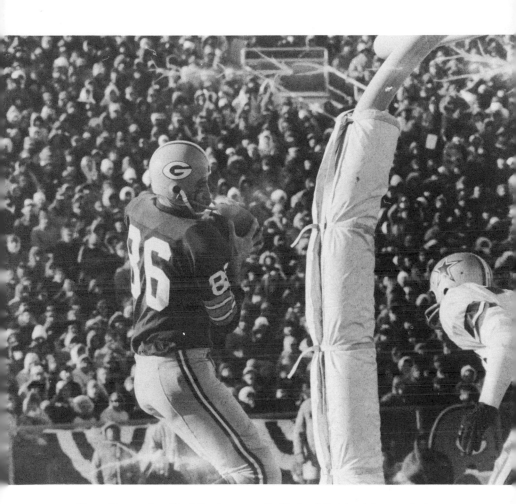

Green Bay receiver Boyd Dowler scores the Packers' first touchdown against Dallas.

eight-yard pass for the touchdown. Then in the second quarter the score escalated to 14-0 on the strength of a "typical" Bart Starr call. The Packers had the ball on the Dallas 43-yard-line, third down and one. The obvious play was a line buck to make the first down. The Cowboys bunched up tight to

stop it. Fullback Ben Wilson took a fake hand-off
and piled into the line, but Starr kept the ball and
dropped back to pass. The fake fooled the Dallas
safety man, Mel Renfro, just long enough for
Starr's top receiver, Dowler, to get behind him.

Starr threw with all his might into a stiff, 15-mile-
per-hour wind. Dowler raced to get under the ball.
It didn't look as if he had a chance. It seemed that
Starr had misjudged Dowler's speed and the wind
and had overthrown the pass. But then the wind
took effect and the ball seemed to hang in the air
waiting for Dowler. He caught it over his shoulder
on the Cowboy 15 and sped into the Dallas end
zone untouched.

The Cowboys were down, but it was too early to
count them out. A year before, in the 1966 championship game, they had fallen behind by two
touchdowns to the Packers. But then they had
staged a thrilling comeback. With less than two
minutes to go they reached the Packer two-yard-
line with a chance to tie the score. Only a clutch interception in the end zone allowed Green Bay to
escape with a 34-27 victory.

Dallas lost the ball on downs after that second-
period kickoff. But then the aggressive Cowboy defense went to work. With the ball on the Green Bay
26, Starr went back to pass. Dallas defensive end
Willie Townes threw him for a 19-yard loss. Bart
fumbled as he was hit, and the other Dallas end,
George Andrie, picked the ball up on the seven-
yard-line and ran over for a touchdown. It was the
first time in the game the Cowboys had thrown

Starr for a loss but it wouldn't be the last. During the afternoon they got to him seven more times for losses of 76 yards. The defense had gotten the first Dallas points and the score was 14-7.

The aggressive Dallas defense catches up with Bart Starr.

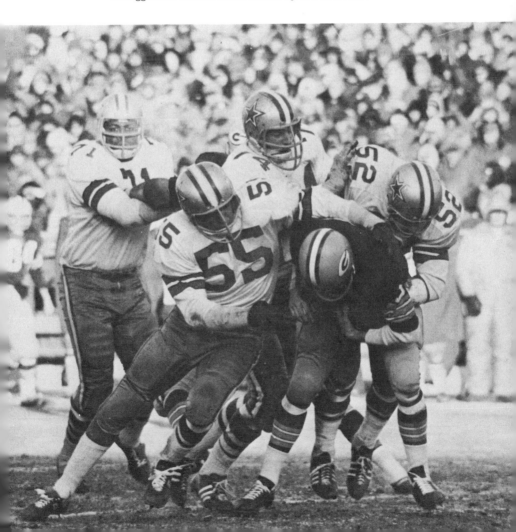

Shortly before the first half ended, the Cowboys got more gift points. Packer Willie Wood fumbled a punt on his 17 and Phil Clark recovered for Dallas. Thirty-two seconds before the half ended, Danny Villanueva kicked a 21-yard field goal to bring the Cowboys within four points, 14-10.

During the first half the big disappointment for Dallas was its inability to move the football on offense. Cowboy quarterback Don Meredith was particularly ineffective. Time and again he missed pass receivers who were in the clear.

"My hands grew colder with each drive," Meredith said afterward. "When your hands are as cold as mine were, you can't wing the ball, and you have to wing it; you have to spiral the ball in a wind like that."

During the intermission Meredith did a tailoring job on his uniform. He cut a hole in the front of his jersey so he could thrust his hands inside and warm them against his stomach. Quickly, the Cowboys came alive on offense. Starting on their 11, they marched to the Green Bay 13. But on the last play Meredith fumbled—and Herb Adderley recovered for the Packers. The Cowboys had lost a fine chance to score.

But soon the Cowboys got another chance. Late in the third period Green Bay was forced to punt and the Cowboys took over in excellent field position on their 45. Meredith lashed out in a hurry. On the first play of the fourth quarter, with second and five, he pitched back to halfback Dan Reeves, who ran wide around the Packer left side. It looked like an end sweep until suddenly Reeves braked and raised his right arm. Option pass!

Packer cornerback Bob Jeter was out of position. "I was slow mentally on that play," Jeter said. "We knew all about Reeves' option pass. They've used it a lot. Willie Wood [the Packer safety man] moved up to meet the run and I took a step up, but when I saw Reeves cock his arm I said to myself, 'Oh, my Lord, what have you done?' I tried to get back, but when I saw the ball in the air I knew it was gone."

It was. Reeves' pass was accurate. Cowboy receiver Lance Rentzel caught it near the sideline on the Packer 20 and sprinted over the goal to complete the 50-yard touchdown strike. The point after was good and Dallas went ahead 17-14. The play, called "fire pitch," had worked well for the Cowboys all season. Reeves had tried it eight times, completing five passes to Rentzel for three touchdowns and 245 yards.

The Packers still had plenty of time, but what happened in the next ten minutes did nothing to encourage Green Bay and its frozen fans. The next two times the Packers had the ball, they gained a total of 21 yards—14 of them on a pass interference penalty.

Then, with five minutes to go, the Green Bay defense held. Dallas was forced to punt and the ball rolled dead on the Packer 32. Suddenly the Packers were the underdogs. They had started out as favorites and taken an early lead. But now they had their backs to the wall, behind with less than five minutes left, fighting the strong Cowboy defense and the sub-zero temperature.

With 4:54 left to play, Green Bay took over on its 32-yard-line. "If we're going to do it," Starr remembered thinking, "it has to be now."

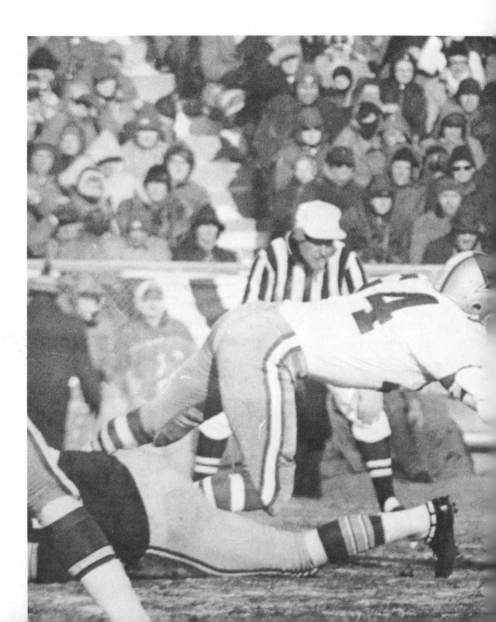

After one running play Starr began to pass. He hit halfback Donny Anderson for six yards. Then

Packer running back Donny Anderson carries the ball.

he tried a run. Fullback Chuck Mercein went
around right end for seven yards as the Cowboys'
quick outside linebacker, Chuck Howley, was blot-
ted out of the play. Then it was back to the air.
Flanker Boyd Dowler cut over the middle and
Starr drilled him with a 13-yard completion.

Then one play almost wrecked the Packers. Anderson raced wide, trying to throw an option pass.
But the Dallas "Doomsday Defense," tough and
wise, dropped him for a nine-yard loss. Resource-
fully, Starr fought back. On second down and 19,
he looped a pass to Anderson over the onrushing
Cowboy linemen and Donny skidded for 13 yards,
down to the Cowboy 30. With two minutes to play
the tension was mounting. It was clear that the
Packers would not get another chance.

The next play was a pass into the flat. Mercein
caught it and made a great individual effort. He
evaded a tackler who could have stopped him for
little or no gain and roared 19 yards to the Dallas
11. Just as important, he stopped the clock by
going out of bounds. Later, Starr explained that
Mercein had not been his primary receiver. "But if
the linebacker doesn't pick Chuck up immediately
when he comes out into his pattern, then I hit him.
I saw the linebacker freeze this time, so I hit Mercein quick. He made the rest of it on his own."

Cowboy linebacker Howley had a different ex-
planation. "There was no traction," he said. "The
advantage had gone to the offense."

With first and ten on the Dallas 11, the Packers
came up with yet another key play. Starr called

what the pros refer to as a "sucker play." When the
ball was snapped, left guard Gale Gillingham
pulled out of the line and went to his right, as he
would do on a sweep to the right. The great Cowboy tackle, Bob Lilly, was "suckered" into following Gillingham to cover the sweep. Lilly left a
fatal hole in the heart of the Dallas line. Mercein
took the ball through the hole for an eight-yard
gain to the Cowboy three.

With 54 seconds to go Starr called time. When
play resumed he sent Anderson off right guard.
Donny gained two yards, enough for a first down
on the one. Again Starr called Anderson's number.
This time the 215-pound halfback hurtled over left
guard—to be met solidly by the middle of the Dallas line. No gain. Twenty seconds left. Starr, famed
for his willingness to repeat a play, went to Anderson again. But the footing was treacherous. Anderson slipped and fell for no gain. Starr signaled for
his last time out. The big clock showed 16 seconds
to play.

"It was time for a big decision," remembered
Starr. "What should we do? Should we run another
play in an attempt to score the winning touchdown? If we failed, would we still have time to attempt the game-tying field goal on fourth down?
Probably not. Or should we play it conservatively,
forget about that extra running play and try a field
goal right then and there, on third down? What
would you have done?"

Starr walked to the sideline to confer with Green
Bay's famous head coach, Vince Lombardi. The

decision they made would determine the outcome of this classic game. No matter how it ended, it would be a kind of upset. If Dallas held on, they would get credit for stopping the favored Packers. If Green Bay won—even though they were favorites—their last-minute comeback against the great Cowboy defense would qualify as an upset. The proud Packers had been pounded and punished for 40 minutes of this game. And just when it seemed that their cause was lost, Green Bay had marched to the Dallas one-yard-line. The next play would decide whose upset it would be.

But let's return to quarterback Starr. "Neither coach Lombardi nor I had any intention of settling for a tying field goal that would take us into a sudden-death period," he said. "We meant to win it in regulation time. But before considering what play to call on that important third down, Coach was interested in the condition of the field. The ground was frozen so hard that we could not get a foothold with our cleats. It was hard for our runners to accelerate and hard for our linemen to make their blocks with authority. Everybody was slipping and sliding.

"Both coach Lombardi and I felt we would have to run the ball over the goal line," Starr continued. "A pass play seemed too risky. But which running play should we use? A dive play, which calls for one-on-one blocking, with the ball-carrier running to whatever daylight opens up? Or a wedge play, which calls for the runner to follow a three-man wedge of blockers straight into the line? We had

Vince Lombardi, dressed for the bitter cold, watches from the sidelines.

run the wedge earlier in the game, and it had worked."

There was much at stake—a third league championship, $8,000 for each winning player and the chance to earn $12,000 more in the Super Bowl. For Vince Lombardi, it was his last chance as Packer coach. Before the next season he would retire from coaching for an office job with the Packers. Yet Lombardi did not tell Starr which play to call. He simply said, "Ask the linemen which play they can execute best and use that one."

Starr returned to the huddle and consulted his linemen. They felt that wedge blocking would be best. Now Starr examined the Dallas front four. He quickly decided against running at the Cowboys' right side. That meant running at All-Pro defensive tackle Bob Lilly. "If Lilly was not the best tackle in football," Bart later explained, "he was close to it. Lilly came in hard and low. Wedge blocking would not work on him."

Then Starr sized up the Dallas left tackle, 6-foot-6, 260-pound Jethro Pugh. The Packers knew Pugh was a fine young lineman, but he had only been in the league two years, so he lacked Lilly's experience. And the films showed that Jethro did not charge as low as Lilly. "I decided that we would have to take our chances running at Pugh," Starr said.

Looking at the frostbitten faces huddled around him, Bart turned to All-Pro right guard Jerry Kramer. Jerry would be primarily responsible for dislodging Pugh. "Can you get enough footing?" the quarterback asked. Kramer's answer came quickly: "I can and I will." So Bart Starr called a play listed as 31-Wedge. Fullback Chuck Mercein would take the hand-off from Starr and try to carry the ball through. Starr slapped his hands together. "We darn well better make it," he said as the Packers broke out of their huddle.

But as he got ready to bark signals, Starr hesitated mentally. He recalled thinking, "What if Mercein slips and doesn't reach the hole on time?" In that split second, Starr recalled a similar situation the year before. On that occasion he had changed his mind at the last moment, kept the ball and scored the touchdown. Before the play started, he decided to keep the ball again.

Kramer, with a big assist from center Ken Bowman, budged Pugh just enough for Starr to lunge over the goal line. The Packers had done it—the championship and a place in the second Super Bowl was theirs. The final score was 21-17.

Green Bay went on to wallop the Oakland Raiders in the Super Bowl, but the year's big game had already been played in sub-Arctic Green Bay. The Packers had done the impossible in the face of the weather, the clock, and one of the finest defenses in football.

"This was it, this was our greatest one," Lombardi kept saying after the game.

The writers asked why Lombardi had risked that last play—he might have ordered a field goal that would have tied the game and sent it into sudden-death overtime.

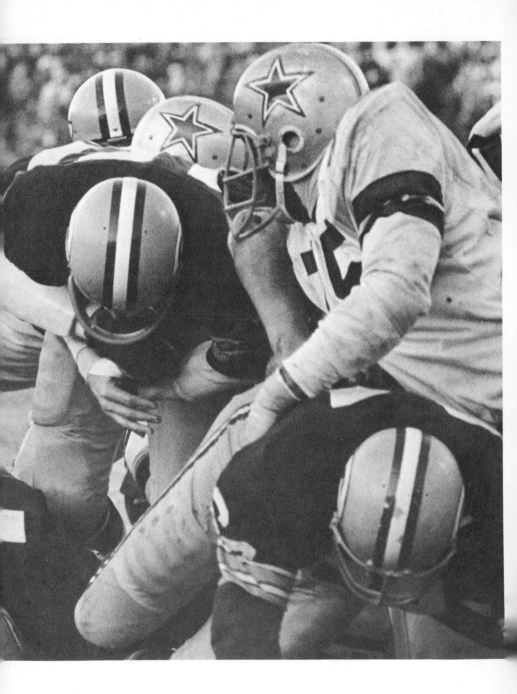

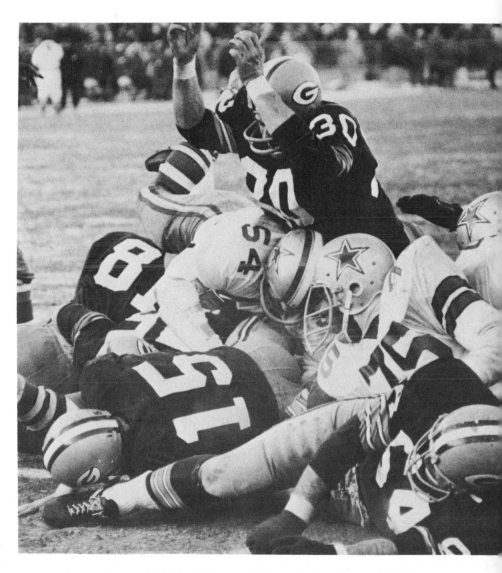

On opposite page, Bart Starr drives toward the goal as Jerry Kramer (striped helmet, lower right) makes the key block. A few seconds later (above), Starr (15) is across the goal with the winning touchdown. Kramer is at lower right.

Vince Lombardi laughed. "Because I didn't want all those freezing people up in the stands to have to sit through sudden-death overtime. That just goes to show that I'm not without compassion, although I'm often accused of lacking it."

Then Lombardi turned serious. "I just got stubborn," he said. "I told them that if they couldn't put the ball into the end zone they didn't deserve to be NFL champions."

9.

NEW ORLEANS vs. DETROIT, 1970:

A Long Kick Takes the Lions' Share

In their early years the New Orleans Saints were never contenders in the NFL. Organized for the 1967 season, they finished no higher than third in their division in their first five seasons. Yet the Saints soon earned a reputation as spoilers. In 1968, for example, they upset the Super Bowl–bound Minnesota Vikings 20-17, and in 1971 the Saints knocked off the future Super Bowl champion Dallas Cowboys 24-14. But probably no victory in the Saints' short history was quite as dramatic or satisfying as the one over the Detroit Lions on November 8, 1970.

By any reasonable judgment, the Saints had no business winning that football game. For one thing, their coaching staff was in disarray. Their head coach, Tom Fears, had just been dismissed, and the Detroit game was the first NFL contest for J. D. Roberts, the new head man.

The Detroit Lions were trailing the Minnesota Vikings by only one game in the Central Division race, and were considered one of the powerful

New Orleans' new coach, J. D. Roberts, talks with substitute quarterback Ed Hargett during the Detroit game.

clubs in the NFL. By contrast, the Saints had won only one game and tied one in their first eight games. Any reasonable man had to favor the Lions. But it has often been said that on any given Sunday, any NFL team can defeat another—regardless of the standings and previous records. This was that "given Sunday."

The only surprising thing about the first three quarters was that the score remained so close. The game played by the Lions was less than elegant. They committed five turnovers. Quarterback Bill Munson had two passes intercepted. Safety man Nick Eddy had fumbled two New Orleans punts and another fumble had cost the Lions the ball again. Each time the Saints recovered a Lion fumble, they went on to score on a field goal by kicker Tom Dempsey. Tom kicked one from 29 yards to open the scoring and put the Saints ahead 3-0. Then, after Mel Farr scored a touchdown for the Lions, Dempsey booted a 27-yard field goal with 15 seconds left in the first half. Thus New Orleans trailed by only one point at the half. The score was 7-6.

Detroit pushed its lead to 14-6 at 9:27 of the third quarter on a two-yard scoring pass from Bill Munson to tight end Charlie Sanders. Then the Saints came back, driving deep into Lion territory. But the drive stalled at the one-yard-line. The crowd booed coach Roberts when he sent Dempsey and the field goal unit onto the field on fourth down at the one. They felt that the Saints should have gone for six points. But Dempsey kicked an eight-yard field goal, making it 14-9, Lions.

Dempsey seemed to have no business playing professional football. Tom had the size, all right— he weighed 270 pounds. But he was afflicted with severe physical handicaps. He had been born with only half a right foot and with a stub for a right hand. Yet Dempsey had refused to let his handicaps conquer him. He played defensive end in high school and college, served his apprenticeship as a minor-league field-goal specialist, and then got his chance with the rebuilding Saints. The league permitted him to wear a special shoe on his deformed right foot.

The heroics began in the fourth quarter. Detroit's Bill Munson threw his third interception of the day and New Orleans linebacker Jackie Burkett brought it back to the Lion 34. Nine plays later halfback Tom Barrington went over from the four. Dempsey kicked the extra point and New Orleans led 16-14 with 8 minutes left.

But the Lions were not so easily defeated. Substitute quarterback Greg Landry piloted the Lions downfield with time running out. With 14 seconds left and the ball on the New Orleans 10-yard-line, Landry called time out. Then Errol Mann kicked a field goal from 18 yards out to give the Lions the lead 17-16. The writer who records the official play-by-play in the New Orleans press box felt that Mann's kick had finished the game, for he wrote that the Lions "went 86 yards in 17 plays to the winning points."

But it was not so easy.

In the eleven seconds left to them after Mann's kick, the Saints had to travel the length of the field against the second strongest defense in the league, and score one way or another. The events of those final seconds were so melodramatic that if they had happened in a movie, no one would have believed them.

After Mann's successful field goal, the Lions had to decide how to kick off. Should they attempt a low, bouncing squibber—to reduce the chance of a long touchdown return? Or should they simply tell Mann to kick the ball as far downfield as he could? Detroit's head coach, Joe Schmidt, chose the long kick. "We wanted to kick off as deep as we could," he said.

Mann got off a respectable kick into a wind of five miles per hour, but it did not reach the end zone, where it could be touched down and brought out to the New Orleans 20. New Orleans' Al Dodd fielded the ball on the 14 and returned it 14 yards to the 28, going out of bounds to stop the clock. The kickoff return consumed only three seconds. Eight seconds were left to play.

New Orleans quarterback Bill Kilmer opened with a sideline pass to the left. Veteran Lion defensive back Dick LeBeau covered wide receiver Dodd closely, but Dodd nevertheless made a magnificent diving catch of Kilmer's pass 17 yards upfield and bellyflopped out of bounds. The play took six seconds and brought the ball to the New Orleans 45.

With only two seconds standing between his

team and another defeat, rookie coach Roberts
faced his first big NFL decision. What should he
do? Try to hit on a long pass? Not likely to work.
Detroit's excellent, experienced pass defense was in
a "prevent" formation designed to stop the long
pass. A screen pass or run? Chances were that neither maneuver would carry the Saints all the way.
And with only two seconds to go, they had to go all
the way in one play or lose the game.

Roberts made up his mind. He sent the hulking
Tom Dempsey onto the field for a desperation field
goal attempt. It was a big risk—the longest field
goal ever kicked in an NFL game had been 56
yards. Dempsey's attempt, from eight yards behind
the line of scrimmage, would have to travel 63
yards. Now Tulane Stadium, the Saints' home field,
resounded with cheers as the crowd of 66,910 realized what Dempsey was going to try.

The snap from center Jerry Sturm spun hard, low
and true into the hands of holder Joe Scarpati, a
veteran pro. Scarpati set the ball down deftly on
the Saints' 37-yard-line. Dempsey took his 2½-step
approach, and dug his stump of a right foot deep
into and under the football. He got plenty of height
on the kick, lofting the ball. Now the same five-
mile-per-hour wind that had shortened Errol
Mann's kickoff gave Dempsey's kick an extra boost
toward the goal posts.

Actually, Dempsey altered his technique slightly
because of the tremendous distance he would have
to propel the ball. "I tried to do it like a kickoff," he

explained later. "I started with my left foot six
inches back of where it is on a regular field-goal
kick—to get more leg swing. I knew the second I'd
hit it that I'd hit it hard. But whether I'd hit it hard
enough to go straight that far, I didn't know."

If Dempsey was dubious, Lion coach Schmidt
was not. "When they lined up to kick, I said there's
no way he's going to kick it. Then I saw that thing

Tom Dempsey begins his 63-yard field goal attempt.

going higher and higher. Then I knew it would carry, but I thought it was going to be wide."

The gun sounded, ending the game, while Dempsey's kick was still soaring through the air. Players on both teams froze in suspended animation. They turned and gazed like tourists looking at the Empire State Building for the first time. They watched the ball carry and carry and carry—until, finally, it tumbled through the lower right-hand corner of the space between the uprights. The referee threw both hands into the air. The kick was good! It was not good by much, clearing the crossbar by approximately three feet, but it was good enough. Tom Dempsey had kicked the longest field goal ever kicked in the NFL. The Saints had won the game 19-17.

Joe Schmidt turned and walked despondently to the locker room, scarcely believing what he had seen, while the New Orleans crowd turned the field into a madhouse. "The guy won the game with a miracle," Schmidt said. "It's like winning the Masters golf tournament with a 390-yard hole-in-one on the last shot." To which Detroit linebacker Wayne Walker added, "It's hard to understand. It was like Bobby Thomson's home run. Nothing compares to it."

The sportswriters later pointed out that Detroit had lost its own game. Detroit quarterback Greg Landry had called time out with 14 seconds left, to set up what looked like the winning field goal. The Saints had gotten the ball with 11 seconds left and had time for two plays. If Landry had only waited

Dempsey follows through as holder Joe Scarpati watches the flight of the ball.

a few more seconds before calling time, the Saints never would have gotten their chance.

But who could have anticipated a 63-yard field goal?

Curiously, the losers that day (Detroit) eventually turned out to be winners in the long run, while the upset winners (New Orleans) might as well have finished their season with Dempsey's kick. The Lions fell two full games behind the Minnesota

Seconds after his record-breaking kick, Dempsey is carried off the field on his teammates' shoulders.

Vikings and never caught up. But they got into the post-season playoffs anyway as the second-place team with the best record (10-4). As for the Saints, they didn't win another game all season.

Just as the Saints went downhill from that epic game, so did big Tom Dempsey. He finished the year as only the 11th best field goal kicker in the league, with 18 scores in 34 tries. The Saints were particularly dissatisfied with Dempsey's record from medium range. Tom made only one out of five field goals from between the 30 and the 39.

Before the 1971 season began the Saints cut Dempsey from the squad. Later in the season Philadelphia Eagle coach Ed Khayat signed Dempsey to a contract. Tom proved to be the NFL's most accurate field-goal kicker, making 12 of 17 attempts.

No matter what happens to Tom Dempsey in the future, they can't take away from him that thrilling day in 1970 when he kicked the king of field goals. He may be cut from an NFL roster. But only another place-kicker can cut Dempsey from the record book. And that will take 64 yards of doing.

10.

NEW ENGLAND vs. MIAMI, 1971:

A Rabbit Pulls One Out of the Hat

Place-kicker Charlie Gogolak of the New England Patriots approached the ball sideways, soccer-style, and hoisted the opening kickoff toward the Miami Dolphins' deep receivers standing on the goal line. The Patriots' home crowd of 61,457 cheered with anticipation as the ball descended into the arms of Miami scatback Eugene "Mercury" Morris on the six-yard-line.

Suddenly, however, the fans' cheers changed to cries of apprehension. Key blocks opened a path through the red-shirted Patriot defenders and Morris moved into the clear. Shifting into high gear, Mercury outraced the last Patriot defenders and scored. Miami's left-footed kicking specialist, Garo Yepremian, tacked on the extra point. With only 16 seconds gone, the Patriots trailed 7-0. It looked like the beginning of a long afternoon for Patriot fans.

Last time the two teams met, early in the 1971 season, Miami had won 41-3. Few people expected New England to win anyway. It was now late in the 1971 season and the Patriots had won four and lost seven. Miami, on the other hand, had a 9-1-1 record (the best in the league at that time). They had won eight games in a row and a win against New England would clinch a place in the post-season playoffs. The Dolphin offense was the flashiest in the NFL, with its great Bob Griese-to-Paul Warfield passing combination and the grinding ball-carrying of Larry Csonka and Jim Kiick.

Patriot coach John Mazur had bitter memories of the terrific beating the Dolphins had given his team earlier. He had worked hard to find a strategy that would change the outcome of the second game—or at least make it closer. He would rely as usual on stocky Carl Garrett for outside running and on hulking Jim Nance for inside power. But for this game Mazur benched tight end Tom Beer and fielded an offense that put three wide receivers on the field at the same time: five-foot, nine-inch rookie Randy Vataha, and veterans Eric Crabtree and Hubie Bryant. The idea was to make maximum use of spectacular rookie passer Jim Plunkett and to put maximum pressure on the Dolphin defense by flooding their secondary with fast, hard-to-cover pass catchers. Mazur especially wanted to work on Miami's second-year cornerback, Tim Foley.

Stung by Morris' game-starting touchdown run, the Patriots fought back immediately. Plunkett threw seven straight passes, moving the ball from the Patriot 42 to the Dolphin 6. From there the 240-pound Nance pounded off-tackle for the touchdown. Charlie Gogolak kicked the extra point to tie the score at 7-7.

Jim Plunkett stands on the sidelines after throwing a touchdown pass against Miami.

For the second time in the game Gogolak kicked off. The last time a bolt of lightning had struck the Patriots. Now, however, it struck the Dolphins. Kick returner Hubie Ginn fumbled on his 26 and New England linebacker Randy Edmunds, a former Dolphin, recovered. Following Mazur's orders, Plunkett went to work on cornerback Foley. Jim sent Vataha downfield against Foley, Randy squirmed free in the end zone, and Plunkett dropped a 26-yard scoring pass into his hands. Gogolak's kick made it 14-7, Patriots.

Gogolak sent his third kickoff soaring downfield. Ginn, who had dropped the previous kickoff, caught the ball on the Miami 2 and made an excellent runback. He reached his 37, where New England's Don Webb hit him with a crushing tackle. The football popped loose and Bob Gladieux of the Patriots fell on it. Four plays later Gogolak kicked a 37-yard field goal to give New England a 17-7 lead. Amazingly, Bob Griese and the Miami offense had yet to run a play from scrimmage.

In the second quarter the Dolphins scored again when Yepremian kicked a 26-yard field goal. Now Miami was only a touchdown behind, and soon they were on another touchdown drive. The tide seemed to be running in their favor. But just as abruptly the tide ran out. The normally sure-handed Jim Kiick fumbled on the New England 21 and Webb recovered for the Patriots, wrecking the drive. Then Plunkett got his passing game going again—racing against the clock. With 40 seconds left in the half, Gogolak's second field goal, this one from the Miami 35, made the score 20-10.

The Dolphins pulled to within seven points early in the third quarter on a field goal by Yepremian. But halfway through the quarter, the Patriots slashed 78 yards in four plays for the touchdown that put the game out of reach. The drive began tamely enough on the Patriot 22 as Plunkett hit Vataha with a sideline pass for a two-yard gain, then overthrew fullback Nance on a swing pattern. But on third and eight, Plunkett spotted Vataha over the middle. The pass covered more than 40 yards and Vataha caught it at the Dolphin 38. He was knocked down at the 25.

New England's Randy Vataha holds the ball high after catching one of his touchdown passes.

The next play was another pass to Vataha. Once again Randy was wide open, this time in the end zone. Miami defenders Jake Scott and the unfortunate Foley had gotten their signals crossed. Each thought the other would cover Vataha deep. As a result, neither did—and the Patriot flanker made a leaping catch of Plunkett's 25-yard pass for his second touchdown of the afternoon. The amazing Patriots led 27-13.

Now the Dolphins were desperate. Starting from the Miami 31, Morris went around right end for nine yards. Then Kiick went wide left for three yards and a first down on the Dolphin 43. Trying to go for it all on one play, Griese aimed a pass for end Howard Twilley. Instead, Patriot defender Larry Carwell intercepted on the New England 47 and ran 53 yards for the touchdown. Gogolak's point-after made it 34-13.

Now in the fourth quarter there was little doubt that the game would be an upset. But the Patriots weren't willing to give up. Miami moved the ball to the New England 9. With first down and goal to go, Morris gained five yards on a run around right end. Then Csonka hit the left side for two yards. But the Patriots were offside. Miami accepted the penalty, the ball was set down on the New England two-yard-line and it was still second down.

Miami's jumbo backs tried again. Kiick, a slashing, driving halfback, gained one yard before linebacker Jim Cheyunski met him head-on. Then Kiick carried again, and Cheyunski slammed into him again—this time stopping the play for no gain.

On fourth down, with the ball approximately a foot away from the New England goal line, the 235-pound Csonka hurtled into the left side of the line. He was hit solidly by linebacker Ed Weisacosky, and when they untangled, the football was still a foot from the Patriots' goal. New England had held! The game ended with the Patriots on top 34-13.

That mighty stand showed how the Patriots managed to control the Dolphin running attack all day long. Csonka was the AFC's second-ranking rusher in 1971, and Kiick finished ninth. But against the Patriots on this afternoon, Csonka and Kiick were able to gain only 76 yards in 18 carries.

"It was," said New England's coach Mazur, "as good a game as we've ever played. And it was no fluke. We didn't make mistakes—no fumbles, no interceptions, no killing penalties."

There was no doubt who the heroes were for the Patriots: Plunkett and Vataha. The upset came as a birthday gift to both. Plunkett, who was later voted the league's Rookie of the Year, celebrated his 24th birthday by completing 16 of 23 passes for 223 yards. Jim had been the NFL's No. 1 college draft choice in 1971. He had begun his rookie season in No. 1 style, leading New England to an upset victory over the AFC's defending Western Conference champions, the Oakland Raiders, and now, in the Patriots' final game of the season, Plunkett went out in No. 1 style by knocking off the powerful Dolphins.

But the game ball did not go to Plunkett. It went

Plunkett fires the ball just as a Miami defender leaps at him.

to the tiny Vataha. Randy had turned 23 the day
before the game—and the icing on his birthday
cake consisted of seven pass receptions for two
touchdowns and 129 yards. Vataha's success dem-
onstrated again that while size is important to a pro
football player, there are exceptions. Giving Vataha every benefit of the doubt, he stood 5-foot-9
and weighed 170 pounds. At Stanford, where he
was Plunkett's pet target, Randy's small stature
and darting moves earned him the nickname "Rab-
bit."

So little that he once got a summer job playing
one of the Seven Dwarfs at Disneyland, Vataha
had been picked in the very last round of the draft
by the receiver-rich Los Angeles Rams. When the
Rams cut him, the Patriots picked him up—mainly
on Plunkett's recommendation. Randy proved
Plunkett's recommendation good by finishing third
among all AFC receivers with 51 catches. He was
outranked only by two great veterans, Fred Bilet-
nikoff of Oakland and Otis Taylor of Kansas City.

In the first flush of unexpected victory, Vataha
put the game into perspective. "All week long," he
said, "I kept remembering that we lost to Miami
41-3 two months ago—and I had the worst day of
my pro career. More than anything else in the
world I wanted to make up for that today."

Randy said that he thought Mercury Morris'
touchdown run with the opening kickoff had ig-
nited the Patriots. "It would have been easy for us
to lay down and die after that," Vataha said. "The
fact that we came right back and scored, and then

won the game, shows the kind of guys we have on this football team."

Miami was hampered by the fact that its star quarterback, Griese, was below par with an injured left shoulder. Griese completed 6 of 12 passes for 70 yards, and had to be replaced in the third quarter by backup quarterback George Mira. But Griese said, "My shoulder isn't the reason we lost today."

Dolphin fullback Larry Csonka cited what he felt was the real reason for his team's defeat: "They beat the devil out of us today."

Csonka felt that the Dolphins had been a bit too confident of their ability to beat the Patriots. In preparing for the game, the Miami players had studied films of New England's defeat by the woebegone Buffalo Bills. "We knew we needed to beat the Pats," Csonka said sadly, "but it's human nature, I guess. After watching the Patriots on those Buffalo game films, we just couldn't make ourselves get up for them."

Indeed, the Dolphins were flat—as their five turnovers (three fumbles and two interceptions) showed. But the great Dolphin linebacker Nick Buoniconti felt that it wasn't all his team's fault.

"Give the Patriots credit," he said. "This was a total victory for them. They really played terrific football against us. They were hitting hard and causing those fumbles. Those things just didn't happen." (They especially didn't just happen to the possessive Dolphins, who in 11 previous games had committed only 15 turnovers!)

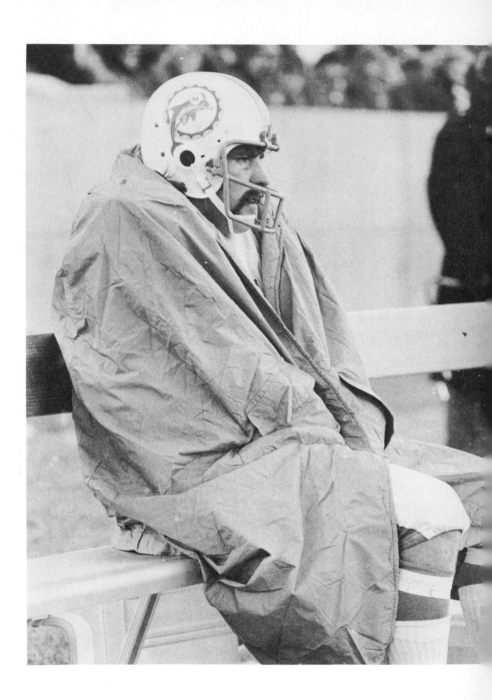

Buoniconti, who spent most of his pro career playing for the Patriots before being traded to Miami, did not think that Dolphin overconfidence or New England's three wide receiver offense had been decisive. "The key was Plunkett having a very big day. He waited until the last split second to release his passes, then hit open receivers." To which New England's general manager Upton Bell added, "You can't throw a football better than Plunkett did today."

But of all the post-game appraisals, perhaps the most important for the future of the Patriots was that given by outside linebacker Steve Kiner. "It's the first game we've won as a team," Kiner said. "In our other victories, either the offense or defense won it—and our specialty teams did nothing. Today was the first time all three units contributed to the total. Yes, the special teams gave up that touchdown on the opening kickoff. But then they bounced back a few minutes later to jar two fumbles loose on the next two kickoffs to set up ten quick points and give us the lead. The offense was great the way it controlled the ball. And the defense came up with some big plays—like that great goal-line stand. That was really something to stop running backs like Csonka and Kiick on three cracks from inside the two-yard-line."

For Miami, the upset was galling but not fatal. The Dolphins went on to make the playoffs by

Miami running back Jim Kiick sits on the bench as time runs out on the Dolphins.

scoring a big win over the Baltimore Colts. Then they met the Kansas City Chiefs for the AFC title. For the Patriots, however, it was a big win. When a team rebuilds, as the Patriots were doing, such a victory can provide a tremendous boost to players not that accustomed to winning. It might also have been the game in which Jim Plunkett came of age, reading the tough Miami zone defense and picking it apart. Some day, when the Patriots are a championship team, the experts will search for the day they turned the corner. They need look no further than December 5, 1971—the day they beat the Dolphins.

Index